Acts Of Kindness

ACTS OF KINDNESS

How To Create A Kindness Revolution

Meladee McCarty and
Hanoch McCarty

Health Communications, Inc.
Deerfield Beach, Florida

Library of Congress Cataloging-in-Publication Data

McCarty, Meladee
Acts of kindness: how to create a kindness revolution/ Meladee McCarty, Hanoch McCarty.
p. cm.
ISBN 1-55874-295-6 (trade paper): $10.00
1. Kindess. I. McCarty, Hanoch. II. Title.
BJ1533.K5M37 1994 93-47019
177′.1—dc20 CIP

ISBN 1-55874-295-6

Publisher: Health Communications, Inc.
3201 S.W. 15th Street
Deerfield Beach, FL 33442-8190

Cover design by Andrea Perrine Brower
Cover needlepoint by Melanie Zinn

To my father and mentor, Eric H. Spiess, for his many acts of kindness to his family and his community. In a quiet way, Eric has helped nearly everybody in our town.

— ***Meladee***

To my great friend, Frank Siccone, whose intelligence, skill and imagination have always been at the service of helping others. I am so grateful for his many acts of kindness.

— ***Hanoch***

Acknowledgments

The authors acknowledge gratefully the help of many good friends and colleagues whose encouragement made this book possible: Gary Seidler and Peter Vegso whose belief in this project was central to its completion. Barbara Nichols, our inestimable editor, whose wit, warmth and wisdom (and irrespressible sense of humor) added immeasurably to its quality. Christine Belleris for her caring and concerned copy editing.

We are especially grateful to Sidney B. Simon for his constant barrage of suggestions, ideas and newspaper articles, and to Suzanne Simon for her many ideas and unflagging support.

Our friends Anne Quinn and Janice Blackwill were great sounding boards with whom we tried out many ideas. Thanks to all the many people whose acts of kindness inspired us every day.

This book is about experiencing more joy in your life by connecting to loved ones, friends, coworkers and anyone else. Not only is an act of kindness good for the other person, it can have major health benefits for you as well.

When we get caught up in the stresses of daily living, or when we encounter challenges, discouragement can set in. An act of kindness can reverse our perceptions of those events and help to refocus us from our troubles to our goodness. It allows healing to begin and brings back meaningfulness to our lives.

An act of kindness to others
can begin our own healing process.

Contents

Introduction

Before you race out to perform an act of kindness, there are a few basic ground rules to consider if you want to make sure that what you plan will have the desired effect.

Ethics And Responsibilities For Acts Of Kindness

1. The act must be safe for you and the recipient.
2. Consider your personal boundaries of comfort and appropriateness and those of the recipient before you choose an act of kindness.
3. Remember, if it is too self-sacrificing, it may lead to resentment. Make sure that your act of kindness is not done in a way to create obligations, dependency, or other negative feelings. It's important not to become a gratitude collector.
4. Ask yourself, "Could this act of kindness go against the receiver's will?" Sometimes, an attempt to be kind may impose our needs on the receiver. Try to do for the receiver what she or he really would want.
5. Might the act embarrass the recipient? Can it be done in a way to eliminate or diminish that embarrassment?

6. Prepare by asking yourself:
   What is it that I want to *do*?
   What do I want to *get* from doing it?
   How do I have to *be* in order to make this work?
7. If your act of kindness is directed at a particular group (the homeless, a cultural group, persons with disabilities, etc.) be sure you're not just projecting your understanding, based on your own life, onto others who may be in very different situations. Try to learn about the group's special experiences and unique point of view. Talk to those people for whom you're planning your act of kindness and learn their feelings about the challenges they face. By tuning up your sensitivity you can be more productive. Never let an act of kindness be patronizing.

Is It More Blessed To Give Than Receive?

We've heard 'tis more blessed to give than to receive, many times, but is it true? Giving is important, but it's crucial to remember that it is an act of kindness to allow someone to give to you. It's important to be a receiver. We need receivers to make giving possible.

Most people say its easier and more comfortable to be a giver. Few of us like to feel beholden. Most people would respond quickly if asked for a favor, but would feel reluctant to ask for one.

It's blessed to be a receiver, too. It's blessed to let someone give to you and for you to receive their gift with grace, gratitude and appreciation. It's blessed to receive without criticism, overt or implied. It's blessed to receive with joy, delight and a child-like spirit.

Why Be Kind? What's In It For Me?

If you're not convinced that acts of kindness are for you, consider the benefits. They should counteract any awkwardness you might feel in reaching out to others.

- Someone will be grateful.
- Enlightened self-interest: people will be kind in return and like you more.
- Mystical self-interest: what goes around, comes around.
- Self-esteem: when you're kind, you like yourself.
- It softens your world: people around you feel more relaxed, kinder, gentler.
- High-level ethics: it's the right thing to do.

Unconditional Acts Of Kindness

Acts Of Kindness

In the Middle Ages, the Jewish sage Moses Maimonides wrote about the seven levels of charity. All of the levels are important, but the highest level of charity is to give unconditionally, anonymously, just because it is right to give. Give a gift, big or small, without knowing who the receiver is and without the receiver knowing who you are.

Toll For Two

Unconditional acts of kindness give us a sense of euphoria, better than alcohol, chocolate or a runner's high.

One of my favorite acts of kindness is to pay for someone's toll fare going over a bridge. I simply pay for myself and tell the toll booth attendant that I'd also like to pay for the friend behind me.

The closest bridges to me are the Golden Gate and Bay Bridges in San Francisco. The city is near and dear to my heart. It gives me great pleasure to start off my day or evening going over one of the bridges and paying for another person. It connects me to another person in a giving, unconditional way. I don't look back to see who receives it. Just knowing that they got it is enough of a good feeling for me. If someone is traveling with me, the act of kindness never fails to bring smiles to my companion — two acts of kindness in one!

Rose On The Windshield

One morning as I was making my rounds of schools as an education consultant, I noticed something very colorful on my car's windshield. As I got closer, I saw that it was a beautiful yellow rose touched with dew. This sight, coupled with the morning sunshine, made me feel warm, physically and emotionally. There was no note attached to the gift.

This act of kindness is one that ranks high for me. The giver couldn't have known what a boost it gave me and couldn't have predicted how many times I would place an anonymous rose on the windshield for unsuspecting receivers.

This unconditional gift of love asked nothing of me. I was so touched that I passed on the kindness as often as I could.

An unconditional act of kindness a day keeps the doctor away.

Do The Wave

As I commute the long distance to my office each morning, the highlight of my trip is the gentleman who waves to me. He walks along the road, rain or shine, facing traffic with his black Labrador retriever. In nine years of commuting, I've consistently gotten a smile, wave and a wish for a good day. What a sweet, endearing, unconditional act of kindness that has been for me. After all these years I don't even know his name, but I take his gift gladly and pass it on because it lifts me so.

Another man in the Boston area gives similar greetings to passersby, lighting one of the corners of that city by sending out greetings of love and endearment. He shakes hands, blows kisses and smiles the most joyous of smiles to anyone, of any color, size, age or economic status.

Two Meals In One

How many times have you watched TV during the holidays and agonized over the long lines of hungry families outside soup kitchens? Often I've felt that the problem is so great that I am powerless to make a difference.

Last Thanksgiving our family planned our holiday dinner, bought twice as much as we needed and then took the second set of dinner ingredients to our local food bank. The administrator told us that the contributions had been lean during the recession. Every little bit did make a difference.

Later that evening, she telephoned to say that a father of four had come to the center in a last effort to see if there was any way he could feed his family that day. He wasn't even thinking of a holiday meal; they were hungry for any food. She said they both cried tears of thanks for our wonderful meal. We were so grateful we'd recognized the opportunity and made the decision to do it again every holiday.

Do Your Job With Quiet Competence

In a world that can frazzle your nerves in an instant, it's always a treat to meet a person who does their job with quiet competence. We have learned to treasure these unsung heroes.

Be that kind of person. Don't wait to be taught. Learn your job. Get really good at it. Find the fun parts. Seize the day! This is your chance to be excellent.

In my travels as a public speaker I've had many opportunities to meet such people and to compare them with others who haven't yet learned the joys of competence. Recently, in a major hotel I saw two desk clerks at the registration desk. One was smiling, greeting each new arrival with eye contact and a cheery, "Welcome!"

Later, I watched her and her partner in a slack moment. This young lady began tidying up, looking for things to do. The other leaned against the back wall, eyes staring vacantly. She said, "Wow, it's so boring here. What a drag." The busy clerk smiled and went on straightening things. She went out and got a fresh basket of apples from the cooler. She came out and looked at the counter from the outside, sizing up how it appeared to a guest. She's going to go far. The other one? Well, she'll probably still be a desk clerk 10 years from now and never know why.

It's a kindness to yourself and to everyone around you to learn your job — and keep learning it. Do it with quiet competence and a sparkle in your eye.

Kind Ways To Celebrate

A Birthday Treasure Hunt

When Bev and I were engaged, I got permission from her roommate to enter her apartment. It was Bev's birthday and she was at work. I hid validations throughout the apartment. Each validation was enclosed in a small, numbered envelope. I knew she would enter her apartment and drop her keys in a small dish. Validation envelope #24 — representing her 24th year — was left there. I hoped she would sense there could be 23 more validations hidden throughout the apartment. I hid the validations everywhere — inside a half-gallon of ice cream (which I knew she would sample before going to bed), under her pillow, inside a shoe, all around her space. At about 1 A.M. I got a wake-up phone call from Bev, reporting enthusiastically that she found all but two of the validations. Where were they?

A dozen years later, I still fondly remember and treasure that experience. And so does Bev.

— *Shared by Jack D. Osman, Ph.D.*

Remember When? Birthday Celebration

Turning a certain age makes some of us feel that youth is lost and the next chapter of life won't be as exciting. As we age, if the future doesn't look as thrilling as the past, our past may become more glamorous.

I have a dear friend whose 40th birthday caused her some discomfort. When her friends gave her the usual humorous old-age birthday cards, it only added to her feelings of loss. Her husband even took her on a cruise and invited seven of her closest friends to help celebrate this passage of time. It was fun but the sense of loss remained, and she struggled with her feelings about it.

Two childhood friends understood her feelings and performed an act of kindness in her honor. They decided to celebrate her youth by taking a trip down memory lane. They got her old cheerleading uniform from her mother, rented a '64 Mustang convertible, and told her she would be going on an adventure of her youth. The only tangible information she had were instructions to be ready at her childhood residence at 9:00 A.M. with a swimsuit and towel. The friends also wore outfits from high school. They drove up to her home in the convertible, playing Beach Boys' music, ready for a typical day of cruising and fun at the beach. They drank cherry Cokes and flirted with guys. They left nothing to chance.

This act of kindness didn't make my friend's feelings of loss disappear, but it contributed to her healing process. Not everyone has a sense of humor about their age. For those who don't, teasing is double torture: once because of the feelings about advancing age, and twice because one is seen as a spoilsport. For these more sensitive friends, what an act of kindness it is *not* to tease.

Happiness is not having what you want,
it's wanting what you have.
— *Unknown*

Birthday Celebrations For A Loved One

Celebrating a loved one's birthday is very significant. For us, it goes beyond the usual Hallmark card.

Here are some ideas for unusual acts of birthday kindness to jump-start your creativity:

- Send birthday wishes from someone famous. For example, "Your political views are right on target. Let us have the opportunity to interview you on *Nightline.* All of us on the news team would like to wish you a happy birthday and many happy returns." Warmly, Ted Koppel.
- Before it's inflated, slip a message in a helium balloon, saying something like this: "Your presence in my life fills me with joy, constantly lifting my spirits."
- Hire someone from your local high school music department to serenade your loved one with the happy birthday song or music significant to the birthday person. Hire the whole marching band! Have them march down the street right up to the front door playing "Happy Birthday to You!"
- Send a week's worth of birthday cards. If it is a significant birthday, such as their 16th, send your special

teenager one card for each year commemorating the significance of their rite of passage.

- Draw a hot, soothing bath for your loved one, and light some candles near the tub. Include a note that says, "Happy birthday. No one holds a candle to you!"
- Coupons are always fun and affordable. Some examples: "Good for one wash and wax of your car"; "Good for servicing your bike"; Good for your laundry, done with care;" and "Good for the service of your choice, performed with a good attitude."
- Take continuous computer paper (the kind that connects together) and list the birthday person's name at the top. Write this statement under their name, "I love you more than all the chocolate in the candy shop, more than all the stars in the sky, more than all the fish in the sea," etc. Leave a box of felt-tip pens nearby so that other loved ones can work on it. Then wrap the birthday present in the colorful graffiti paper you've created.

A Celebration: An Act Of Extraordinary Kindness

There was a certain sadness as I neared my 60th birthday. I was struck by the possibility that I was no longer a young man, full of promise and hope, a man with an abundant future.

My wife, Suzanne, sensed my feelings and decided to celebrate me in a special way. My birthday came up on a day when we were in Germany where I was conducting a workshop. Suzanne had the day free, and she spent it wandering the nearby forest, collecting — imagine this if you can — 60 different, distinct objects she found in the woods. There was a bird's feather, a piece of moss, a chunk of bark, a snake skin, a wide variety of wild flowers, stones, and on and on and on.

Suzanne spread all 60 of these objects out on the dining room table where we were staying and — imagine this well — wrote out 60 short notes, matching each item she found with one of my characteristics. They were 60 validations written with the most love, tenderness and recognition I had ever known.

"You are like this rock: solid, dependable, immutable and ageless. I love you, Rocky."

"This feather came from a bird that flew high in the air. I watch you fly and see you soar and I know you have flights yet to make. How gloriously you fill my sky."

I think you get the idea.

Now, who do you know with a birthday coming up soon? How can you celebrate that person? Does Suzanne's idea for my 60th birthday give you an idea for your special person?

— *Shared by Sidney Simon*

Birthday Letter To Friends From Friends

There are significant ages in our lives that warrant special celebrations. Our dear friend Suzanne Simon, the "birthday meister," once shared with me the beautiful and unique way she celebrated her daughter's 16th birthday.

Suzanne wrote a special letter to all of her daughter's friends, special family members and significant others. In the letter, she asked them to write a letter in return, sharing words of wisdom: a quote to remember, a good book to read, a favorite joke, an affirmation. She held a birthday party and presented her daughter with an album of all their wonderful letters. It was a treasure beyond her wildest dreams. Her daughter and her friends had a great time poring over the letters, languishing in tears or bursting into laughter at each one.

I was so touched by this act of kindness that I made it a point to adapt it for my mother's 75th birthday, my husband's "49th and holding birthday," and my special friend Anne's 40th birthday. The age is not significant to the act. Possibilities are limitless if you just use your love and creativity.

The following birthday letter asking for letters for my friend Anne's birthday is one example of how to get the birthday book started. The note to friends and family went something like this:

Dear ____________________:

Anne is turning the big 40 this year. Her family and I are planning a little surprise get-together to help celebrate this momentous occasion and we'd love to invite you to join us.

I am enclosing a special birthday letter that I would appreciate your filling out for Anne. Just fill in the blanks with good wishes and humor or be creative and "do your own thing." I am making a covered birthday album to put them all in. Please remember this is not a graded activity. Simply share yourself and your heart-to-heart connection with Anne on paper. She'll adore anything this special from you. Include a picture if you can. If you aren't able to attend the party just slip the birthday letter in the self-addressed envelope and let me know you won't be attending.

Going Out With A Smile

If you're really lucky during your career, you'll work with some very special people. If you're smart, you'll celebrate with them while they work with you. If you want to put your appreciation into action upon their retirement, there's a wonderful way to send them off with a smile and a written validation.

I was fortunate to work with Art. He faced many challenges but came to a turning point that sent him on a journey of giving a little back. He adopted the philosophy of the Serenity Prayer and the commitment simply to be there as a sponsor for 12-Step programs.

You could hear Art whistling three blocks before he reached the office door every day. He never failed to greet me with a warm smile and a kind word. One of his unique qualities is to collect quotes for every occasion, which he often used to lighten the gravity of a difficult situation. My personal favorite is, "If you're on the Titanic, changing seats won't make a difference." With a man like this you can imagine the multitude of folks wanting to pay tribute to his retirement. One of his colleagues, Eddie Martin, along with our brilliant administrative technician Cathy Ryan and a host of other friends and coworkers, went about collecting all of his quotes. The collection ended up as a decoration for the celebration. His quotes were artfully illustrated on a placemat to decorate each place setting. They were such a hit that people took them home as souvenirs and asked for extra copies to share with friends.

Along with each invitation was a request for any photos of Art to be used in the celebration and a special sheet to fill out with caring wishes. These were included in a covered album as a remembrance.

Wedding Rings: Circles Of Love

Celebrations are vital for giving people recognition and letting them know you value them. Special occasions can be great gifts in themselves if done with a true awareness of the uniqueness of the people involved.

Our wedding (the second marriage for both of us) brought two families together. We wanted a way to celebrate the uniqueness of our new family, yet connect them with some type of symbolism indicative of how much we cherished them all. We purchased silver rings for all the children. The girls' rings were a band of children holding hands, and the boys' rings were three interconnected silver bands. As the two of us exchanged rings, we included the four children. Hanoch connected to my children by placing the rings on their fingers, and I connected to his children by placing the rings on their fingers. We had one child, who is a poet, guitarist and song writer, compose a piece for the wedding. Our daughter the artist displayed some of her beautiful work. These are just tiny ways of saying, "You are important to us because of your uniqueness, and we celebrate having you as part of this family."

Kindness Through Music

Once I gave Meladee a Peter Max pin that said "Music Heals" — something we both believe. Because our bodies function biologically in rhythms, people have a sensual and emotional reaction to music. A couple might have that one special piece of music that triggers strong emotions when they hear it. Other music has powerful impact on people, such as the "Wedding March," "Hail to the Chief," the "Marine Hymn" and the "Star-Spangled Banner." Sometimes a song triggers memories of great happiness or sadness. Providing someone you care about with a special piece of music can be a fabulous act of kindness.

Our wedding was special because we were surrounded by friends and family who shared in the celebration. It was a beautiful outdoor wedding, under a bower in a rose garden at a Victorian mansion in California's wine country. The guests all assembled. Classical flute and guitar music of our choosing filled the air with a melodious tribute to our love. A processional welcomed each member of the wedding party. We stood in front of the rabbi and nervously but joyously said our vows.

We turned, now man and wife, joined with great hope and happiness. We walked down the aisle past our beaming families and friends. Suddenly, I noticed what the chamber musicians were playing: "Zippedy-Doo-Dah!" I was stunned. I whispered, " 'Zippedy-Doo-Dah?' Is that what you asked them to play?"

My darling bride smiled happily and said, "Want to skip down the aisle, honey?" Skip down the aisle we did.

The light-hearted tune was Meladee's gift to me of a lifetime of humor and laughter as well as serious love.

Songs that can help you to kindly celebrate special occasions from the heart are:

"Seasons of the Heart"
"As Time Goes By"
"Heart to Heart"
"Bridge over Troubled Waters"
"Moon River"
"Don't Walk out on Love"
"This Must Be Love"
"Just the Way You Are"
"Somewhere over the Rainbow"
"You Are So Beautiful"

Add your own special songs to this list. Use your sweetest imagination and hunt for ways to incorporate this music into the special moments of your life.

Treasure Map

Our travels around the world have given us the opportunity to meet many wonderful people. Some of them graciously opened up their homes and hearts to us. In these instances, a simple thank you didn't quite seem enough to express our gratitude for their kindness and generosity.

A teaching assignment in Norway became one of these treasured experiences. We made many close friends during our time there. The Norwegians we met were joyous people whose uninhibited laughter and philosophy of kindness was infectious and unforgettable.

As a special thank you for our trip, we sent our friends a treasure map, consisting of an enlarged version of the country with pictures we'd taken. Each experience was noted on the map with photos and a descriptive narrative of the event. Many of the notations were highlighted with inside jokes and the verses of songs we had sung together.

One song that we learned from our Norwegian friends was "Sang Till Friheten" (translated: "You Are the Finest That I Know"). As a gift to us, our friend Marrit Nesvold translated it into English which we will share with you.

Sang Till Friheten

You are the finest that I know.
You are the dearest in the world.
You are like the stars, like the winds, like the waves, like the birds, like the flowers in the field.

You are my mentor and my friend.
You are my truth, my hope, my love.
You are my blood, my lungs, my eyes, my shoulders, my hands and my heart.

Freedom is your lovely name.
Friendship is your proud mother.
Caring is your brother.
Peace is your sister.
Courage is your father.
The future is your responsibility.

Repeat the chorus: You are the finest in the world.

Birthday Letter To Children

(from Meladee)

I feel very fortunate to be a mother and stepmother. I have experienced some blissful moments in my life as a parent that cannot be matched or repeated. As a new mother I have known the frustration of having more to do than hours in the day permitted. I wanted desperately to record in my childrens' baby books every new skill, date of their first tooth, the day they took their first step, and all of their other firsts. I felt guilty when time passed and I didn't get it all down in writing. Questions kept going through my mind like, "What if something happened to me or my husband and there was no one to remember the special events?"

I decided to purchase a small notepad to keep in my purse. Every time my children said a new word, or performed a new action, I noted it. Once each year on their birthdays, I write them a letter telling them of their accomplishments loved ones, favorite toys and foods, special pictures, friends and special events. As they grow older, I include awards they received, or special things they wrote. Included in my letter to them is an affirmation of their uniqueness, how much I love them, and what they brought into my life this year. I then seal it and place it in their own special file box to be opened on their 21st birthday.

My children are fully aware of their birthday letters. Often they help me write them and say, "Don't forget to include the award for the essay I wrote," or "Don't forget to include that picture of my slumber party."

This birthday letter obviously is as much for me as it is for them, maybe more. It helps me to take stock of the positive highlights of the year. It helps me to remember to look at my children through appreciative eyes. Sometimes we parents get so bogged down with the trivial or negative things our children do, that we forget to focus on the important things like the wonderful, healthy people they are turning out to be. A birthday letter brings it all back into focus for me. It's not so time-consuming that it is drudgery to complete; it flows from the heart. I take simple notes throughout the year to jog my memory.

Sometimes, I must admit, I give in to enclosing free advice or quotes about my life. I'm hoping a quote or saying might fill in life's little values when I forget to do it in person. One of my favorites comes from Colin McCarty:

> Remember these things: Dream it. Do it. And discover how special you are. Be positive, for your attitude will affect the outcome of many things. Ask for help when you need it; seek the wisdom the world holds and hold on to it. Make some progress every single day. Begin. Believe. And become.

Some other thoughts you might weave into a birthday letter, if you're careful not to overdo it, are:

> Give yourself all the credit you're due. Don't shortchange your qualities, your abilities, or any of the things that are so unique about you. Remember how precious life can be. Imagine. Invest the time it takes to reach out for your dreams; it will bring you happiness that no money on earth can buy. Don't be afraid; no mountain is too big to climb if you do it at your own pace.

Hospice Volunteer

A hospice patient, a woman with pancreatic cancer who had but a few months to live, complained about the expense her daughter-in-law had gone to for her grandson's birthday party. Sadly, she couldn't relate to this normal childhood celebration because as a child she had never been given a birthday party. I wanted her to experience the feeling of a celebration in her honor and told her I would give her the perfect party, exactly as she wanted it. Our last months together were spent planning the event down to its final detail. A lifetime of memories came flooding back to her in the process. She even spoke to relatives with whom she'd been out of touch for years.

Planning the party brought my friend great joy and renewed vitality as she experienced things and went places that were previously out of her grasp. One particular incident involved a trip to a bakery noted for its fine pastries. Although the woman had heard of this shop, she'd never gone inside to sample its goods because she could not afford them. When I suggested that we go to the bakery to sample the pastries for her party, she got out of her chair and walked unaided to the coat rack. It was the first time I'd ever seen her walk alone. When we got to the bakery, she walked in, slapped her hand down on the counter and announced to the clerk, "We're having a party!" We ordered orange juice and a sampling of pastries. Although she was too sick to do much more than nibble at the sweets, she didn't stop looking around in total wonderment; no detail of the shop escaped her notice.

On the day of the party, she got up early and dressed in her best suit. Even though it was riddled with moth holes, she was proud to be wearing it. By 7:00 A.M. she positioned herself in her chair and became Queen for the Day.

Every detail of the party had significance for her. In the process of planning it she shared a lot of herself with me, took a lot of risks and had the courage to overcome her fears before it was too late. We celebrated a life that had known loss and disappointment, but the party was the most joyous I've ever been part of. Most of all, I learned a lot about the triumph of the human spirit!

Even a week after the party, this woman who never smiled, because her grim life had given her little to smile about, grinned from ear-to-ear. "I guess we can congratulate ourselves for the party we had!" she said. Her joy was the direct result of fulfilling the very real human need to rejoice and give thanks. She died a few weeks later.

— Contributed by Patricia A. Lorda

Kindness Through Humor And Playfulness

Humor And Playfulness

Be kind to yourself and others with humor and playfulness. Adopting a lighthearted attitude can bring you important benefits:

- It provides perspective. No problem is so great that it can't be overcome. Today's mountains become tomorrow's molehills.
- Others will find you more approachable.
- You'll have more energy because you won't waste it coping with tension.

Remember:

- Be sure the humor is tasteful, or at least doesn't violate the standards of the recipients.
- Don't make someone the butt of your humor. While many people enjoy bantering, others might be threatened, embarrassed, challenged or provoked by it.
- Timing is everything. The funniest joke sours if told at an insensitive moment.

Pollyanna Was Right

Pollyanna, the eternal optimist, was right, always believe the best!

Our view of the world affects our creativity, reception to love and our health, to name a few. Laughter can ease the gravest situations. Humor is valuable. In a recent behavioral study people were asked which they could live without, laughter or sex, in return for a million dollars. Overwhelmingly, sex was the answer.

If you want to give yourself a lift, buy a gift that will keep you giggling: go to your local variety or toy store and purchase some funny glasses. Our favorites are the Groucho Marx variety — with the big nose and mustache attached — because they tickle the nose as well as the funny bone.

The humor quotient for Groucho glasses is limited only by your imagination. For instance:

- Buy a pair of funny glasses for each member of your family and have the family portrait taken with them on. We did this and even included the dog in the picture wearing his own set of glasses.
- Do holiday decorating with lots of funny items. A Christmas tree could have clown noses, Groucho

glasses, bow ties that light up and other whimsical ornaments.

- Leave a pair on display at your desk as a reminder to lighten up. We give ourselves enough stress on the job as it is. Give yourself a daily dose of humor. It increases creativity, decreases stress and promotes retention of learned material.

When somebody dumps all over you for no good reason, resist the urge to get mad or even. Instead, put on your funny glasses while the person is carrying on. It is a healthy way to diffuse a volatile situation and should lighten your load of stress. The following example is a case in point.

Meladee was helping to conduct a school meeting between two angry parents and the school counselor who seemed equally upset with them. The conversation was getting nowhere fast when she had an inspiration. "Would you do something if I asked you to, just as a favor?" she asked the parents.

"What is it?" they asked.

"You'll have to trust me. Would you do it? Take a risk." Intrigued, they agreed.

She turned to the counselor. "And you, would you do it too? Just as a favor?" He, too, was intrigued. And, not wanting to seem uncooperative, he agreed.

She reached into her purse and took out three pairs of Groucho glasses, complete with giant pink noses and bushy black mustaches. "Put these on!" she commanded. Startled and cowed by her beaming but powerful assertiveness, they complied. "O.K., now continue the discussion."

There was a long silence as the adversaries glared through the glasses at each other. Suddenly, they burst into laughter. Because of the tension that had been so intense in the room, the laughter was explosive and long. When it subsided, the tension dissipated.

The father said, "It's damned hard to stay mad wearing these dumb things!"

"I couldn't either," said the counselor.

The discussion, minus the accusatory tone, resumed. They actually came to a good resolution in a remarkably short time.

He who laughs, lasts.
— Mary Pettibone Poole

Additional Ways To Bring More Humor Into Your Life

Leave funny jokes or messages on sugar packets in restaurants. For example: How many presidential aides does it take to screw in a light bulb? Answer: None. They like to be kept in the dark.

Write funny captions near the faces of famous people on magazines or newspapers in your home. It will bring a smile and a giggle to those you live and love with.

Leave humorous reading material, such as Gary Larson's *The Far Side* books, near your phone (for those frustrating times when you're put on hold) or on your coffee table so that a smile is readily available.

Pack a fun kit for your car so you can indulge yourself in laughter, rather than anger, when stuck in a traffic jam. Put on your silly glasses and get a giggle from the occupants in the car next to you. Our glove compartment is stocked with clown noses, various whistles and noisemakers and other props.

Send someone a kaleidoscope. Invite them to look at the glorious colors of the kaleidoscope to see if things shift for the better.

A Spoonful Of Humor Helps The Medicine Go Down

When our family members, friends or colleagues face challenges of illness or injury, we let them know we care enough to want to boost them on to recovery. We shower them with positive thoughts and watch them heal.

Documented medical research shows that positive moods and expectations make us feel better, improves our overall health and increases our longevity. We have a remarkable internal health maintenance system that acts like an emergency electrical generator. When our body stops functioning properly, our brain can kick in to restore our balance and energy. Positive thinking is the switch.

We're not suggesting that a patient hopes for a genie to appear and remove their illness. Instead, we recommend optimism and faith to speed the recovery process. We can rely on our doctor's drugs or electrical stimulation for relief and dulling of the symptoms. Also we have the capacity to turn on our natural pleasure enhancers with good tastes, sounds, smells, sights and sensual experiences.

To keep the laughter and thus the healing process speeding along, invest in some funny audio tapes for a sick friend. Give him a tape player and a set of earphones. Soon his laughter will drown out the beeps and hisses of hospital equipment and the moans and groans of other patients.

Along these same lines, an organization called the Institute for the Advancement of Human Behavior, which is devoted to the role of humor in healing, spirituality and good mental health, provides materials and tapes to boost recovery.

It is when humor restores proportion
that our blind eye is opened.
— *Lorraine Risly*

Acts Of Kindness In Friendship

I Called Her Last!

Sometimes we indulge in a self-defeating game with a friend, called, "I called last." You can even hear a whining little note in the claim. Of course, you really believe that you've been doing all the work of keeping your relationship alive. After all, you send the cards every holiday and birthday; what more can be expected? When weeks go by and you haven't heard from your friend, you begin to sulk inside. You miss her, or feel lonely and make the first call.

When you're together, it's great. Your friend really seems to value and enjoy your company. But when you're apart, it's the old cliche, "Out of sight, out of mind." As the time gap increases, so does the emotional gap. You feel hurt, devalued and disregarded.

"I called her last," you say petulantly. "If she really cared, she'd call." Cobwebs gather on your phone.

At this point, you have to make a decision about keeping the friendship alive by calling or writing, or not reaching out as a matter of principal. You need to decide which is more important, the friendship or to be right. It can be tough to swallow your pride, but if you care about keeping your friendship alive, you'll call. Just imagine how you'd feel if you steadfastly refused to call and then heard your friend had moved away, or worse, had died unexpectedly.

When you have decided to make contact, the phone call or note should begin like this: "I was thinking of you and reflecting about how much I care for and miss you." The note or conversation must not begin with recriminations, just kindness.

If you are a teacher, this is a wonderful idea to share with your students. Bring a pile of stamped envelopes to class. Give them out to your students and actually have them write a heart-felt letter to a friend they've lost touch with. Folks generally come back to class excited about the results.

Networking with people you've had a personal growth experience with can be initiated by doing a one-minute love call. Actually set a timer and call the person, stating, "This is a one-minute love call to let you know I'm thinking of you and appreciate you for ____________." At the end of the minute, thank them, bid them farewell and hang up. Watch, they'll come back soon!

Picnic In The Parking Lot

We all have people in our lives who we'd love to spend more time with, but whose busy schedules make it difficult. Our friend Matthew Weinstein is one of those special people. He is bright, creative and embodies such a wonderful sense of humor and playfulness that people are drawn to him. Unfortunately, Matthew always has a "full plate" and getting together with him calls for creative scheduling.

One of Matt's friends was undaunted by the challenge of fitting into Matt's busy schedule. He found a way to get together with Matt and perform an unusual act of kindness. Matt called to say that he would be traveling through his area but, unfortunately, had only a one-hour layover. Could they get together for a cup of coffee and catch up on old times?

Matt's friend agreed, saying he'd meet him at the arrival gate. There, the friend declined the coffee and escorted Matt to the airport parking lot. At the friend's car, out came a small picnic table, two chairs, a portable tape deck complete with music, a small bud vase with a rose, coffee and appetizers. Soon, the parking lot "disappeared." Matt and his friend feasted, laughed, reminisced and made promises to reconnect. All this caring and sharing took place in less than an hour. Quality, not quantity, is what counts.

Friends And Family In Far Away Places

Remember your first trip to camp? I remember it fondly. Along with all of the camp activities and friends I made, I remember the care package of cookies and letters my sister-in-law sent me. I shared all the goodies and was an instant hit with the other campers, but more, it was the feeling of being valued by someone that stayed with me.

My high-school friend Sharon became an exchange student in Germany during our senior year. I desperately wanted to be an exchange student myself, but didn't feel confident with my foreign-language skills and so succumbed to the safety of home.

I admired Sharon's sense of adventure and risk and wanted to validate those characteristics in her as well as remind her of her friends at home. I gathered photos from the yearbook staff and created a box I covered with a collage made from bits and pieces of fabric, photos, quotes and jokes. In the box, I placed programs from school events, ranging from drama productions to sports teams' standings. I included the school and local newspapers and a couple of Sharon's momentos that I got from her mom.

Sharon received the box at a time when the longing for home was at its greatest. That gesture helped me to feel good about myself, even though I didn't have the courage to make the journey.

There are many special ways to correspond creatively with people you miss in far-away places. Here are a few:

- Glue a special message, caption, photo or newspaper clipping to the back of a piece of cardboard. Make the cardboard into a jigsaw puzzle and send one piece each day or week to your friend or loved one. It is a fun way to show how much you value the person. They will appreciate the effort and look forward to receiving the next piece of the puzzle.
- On special occasions, such as a birthday, anniversary or promotion, send a card with a faux message from someone famous. For example: "I could learn a lot about love from you. Happy birthday," Leo Buscaglia.
- Photo cards are great fun. Find a silly picture of your family or loved one and have it made into a photo postcard — a service available at many photo developing stores. Send a playful message with the card. It will be a nice keepsake.
- Make a tape of your loved one's favorite songs and then add a special message at the end, reminding them that although far away, they are never out of your heart.
- If you are the one traveling away from your family, leave each one of them a love note to open every day

that you're gone. This is a great hit for young children who find it very difficult to cope when parents travel. In each note, include a treat such as a piece of gum or candy. A poem, using the person's name or something unique to them, is also very exciting to receive.

"Chicken Soup" Friend

A "chicken soup" friend is a person who brings you healing nourishment when you're sick. He or she is present physically for you in your time of need.

A group act of kindness is a "dinner chain" — a nourishing meal provided by a different person each evening. To start it, write a note — with a calendar attached — that says something like this:

> As you probably know, Jim is recovering from his operation and has a hard time. Would you join us in support of Jim's healing by providing dinner for him once this month. If you can, sign the calendar on the day you'd like to prepare and deliver a meal to Jim. If you need help delivering it, please let us know and we'll make arrangements.
>
> Jim has special dietary needs indicated below. Please use disposable/recyclable containers so he won't feel the added stress of trying to return them after the meal.

Another act of kindness is to make two casseroles instead of one and take it to a friend, neighbor or shut-in. There is no more effort involved to make two dishes, but the labor of love will go twice as far.

— *Shared by Sid Simon*

Kind Acts For Your Family

Thanks Mom!

Moms are always sacrificing for their children. Think back and remember when your mother did without something so that you could buy that toy you liked so much. Moms are always there when you need them.

While we honor our mother on Mother's Day, she'll feel really special and loved if you celebrate her when she's least expecting it. Try this table-turning move: Send your mother flowers on your birthday, thanking her with a loving note that reads, "Thank you for giving me life. I love you very much."

Just this one, simple act of unexpected kindness is guaranteed to fill your mother with great joy and pride in having raised you to be such a good person.

"It's Your Turn"

A dream of many people who are part of a couple is to share equally small, personal favors such as neck rubs or back scratches. Unfortunately, some folks feel the need to keep score or a balance sheet of, "You owe me," or "It's your turn." Sometimes the kindness of a loving act gets subverted by covert game-playing.

These guidelines can help restore the loving and kindness to this exchange of small, yet intimate, personal favors.

- Give freely, without expecting anything in return.
- When asked for a back scratch or neck rub, oblige willingly and don't sigh. It is a small pleasure and doesn't take much energy.
- Don't require verbal thanks. Assume that your actions are appreciated.
- Let your partner fall asleep. It's a sign that you were effective.
- Don't use the kindness for sexual purposes unless your partner is on the same wavelength. This is a simple act of kindness and you shouldn't be looking for self-gratification.

Keeping A Relationship Alive And Playful

Our friends Rosemary and Harry Wong have a wonderful ritual they practice to keep their relationship alive and playful. Every six weeks they take turns planning some time away together and build this time into their calendars. The partner planning the event keeps secret the playful and creative event.

This is a wonderful way to stimulate communication, foster intimacy and recharge your relationship. The monotony of daily routine can desensitize us. Little adventures, on the other hand, are rewarding because they are stimulating

If you'd like to try this ritual for yourself, keep the information about the plan down to the bare necessities: what to bring, wear and when to be ready. If the spirit moves you, it is allowable to give some clues. A fun way to do this is to send your loved one on a treasure hunt to to discover where you're going. Start by sending her to a bookstore to pick up a copy of a book that has something to do with the surprise.

Here are some fun ideas to boost your creativity and imagination:

- Take a bike trip. Ride the ferry from San Francisco to Angel Island. There is a seven-mile round-trip bike course there with roadside picnic tables. Docents are available on the weekends to give the history of the island. Find a beautiful place near you to bike and picnic.
- Spend a weekend in a cozy cabin in the woods with no phones or televisions.
- Try a full massage treatment. What a wonderful treat to be surprised with a gift certificate for a full body massage. It's both relaxing and invigorating.
- Buy tickets to an outdoor concert.
- Take a picnic and enjoy the sunset.
- Walk on a deserted beach and collect seashells.
- Enjoy a music festival. They are everywhere, if you look. Try some new and adventurous styles of music.
- Attend a clown school. Barnum and Bailey run several of them all over the country.
- Take dance lessons.
- Attend an Earth Day celebration. Numerous cities have celebrations and offer good food, music, crafts and energy-saving ideas.
- Spend an evening at a dinner theater. A new trend in dinner theater that we've found to be a fun experience is the "Murder Mystery Theater." At dinner,

there's a mock murder. Guests spend the evening trying to sort out whodunit.

- Sign up for a big league baseball camp for adults.
- Buy tickets to see a favorite comedian when he or she is in your town.

Don't Go Away Mad!

Not many parents enjoy disciplining their children, but to develop well-adjusted and well-balanced kids you must keep set limits and reinforce consequences. It's not pleasant, but it must be done.

Here are ten steps to bring kindness back into the equation:

1. Take a deep breath and let it out slowly.
2. Count to 10 slowly. This will calm you enough so that you don't give in to the urge to yell or begin a barrage of negative criticism about the infraction — plus all the others he's committed in the past.
3. Be specific. Deal in the present when discussing the problem. Avoid the statements "you always" or "you never."
4. Ask the child to repeat for you the rule he's broken. If it hasn't been an established rule, set the standard and outline the consequences of breaking it so that next time he will make a better choice.
5. Let him tell his side of the story and listen without interrupting.
6. Outline what it is he needs to do to make the situation better, or explain the consequence for the

infraction. Focus on how he can fix what he broke, replace what he used or complete the task he forgot. It's a great kindness to be given a way out of trouble. After all, punishment isn't your goal, is it? Your goal is to teach your child right from wrong and establish good habits and values. To accomplish this, he must be given the chance to repair his errors.

7. Ask him what he will do the next time he is faced with a challenge.
8. Listen.
9. Remind him that it is his action that causes you distress, not he as an individual.
10. Last, and most important, hug him or ask him for a hug when the process is completed. This gives young people the tactile and emotional reinforcement that, no, you didn't like what they did, but they are still lovable and capable, no matter what!

If this is a really serious infraction, sit knee-to-knee with your child, hold hands and talk calmly. Remind your child of how difficult this is for you to experience as well. Use self-disclosure about when you've made a wrong choice. Have the courage to show imperfection and allow it in your child.

It is those times when we least deserve a hug
and support that we need it the most.

— *Glennis Weatherall*

Do Something Without Being Asked

We all are imperfect. That is one of the defining characteristics of being human. With imperfection come errors in judgment — sometimes we are wrong. Others can see our errors because distance gives them perspective. When the tables are turned and our parent, spouse or child is wrong, it is easy to forget our own errors and say, I told you so. Instead, shoulder the blame once in a while even if you don't own it. It costs you nothing and makes the other person feel a whole lot better for not having to relive their mistake. They probably feel bad enough as it is.

Along the same lines, give in every once in a while and let your loved one win an argument or a game. You know you could have won, but this way there are two winners instead of one. Everyone goes away feeling good.

It is a welcome treat, too, for your loved one to find a special job or household duty completed with a note waiting for them that says something like: "I really appreciate you and I wanted to do something for you today," or "Congratulations the Laundry Elf was here to do your wash!"

No act of kindness is wasted.
— William Purkey

The Little Things In Life

The media puts enormous pressure on families to provide their children with expensive trips to amusement parks, the latest $299 athletic shoes and designer clothing.

Every time we get caught up in the price-tag mentality and need a breath of reality, we glance at one of the many quotes we keep handy. This particular quote was given to us by a friend who has a full-time job, a husband, four children and a farm to tend. "The most important thing you can give your children is your time."

So what is her secret? Exactly how does she give her children time when she has so many responsibilities? "Make a *big deal* out of nothing," she said. "I take them on *big outings* and take them to *big places.*"

Your children will remember and appreciate the little things that you turn into a big adventure. Here are some ideas:

- Take your children to parades and the most lovely parks you can find.
- Make a picnic special by packing your children's favorite foods. Bring along a ball, a Frisbee or fun games.

- When doling out your child's allowance, discuss how she will save and what she can purchase. Choice gives her a sense of power. Show her your approval in her decisions.
- Take your family on an excursion to the library or museum so that you can build their level of awareness of life's possibilities.

Many families are on a tight budget, but you can always share with your children the richness that comes in planning and orchestrating an event. Be fully present for them during the experience. Shut down the urge to have your mind on other things.

Make it extra special by including an ice cream soda afterward, or bring real champagne glasses and toast the celebration with sparkling apple cider. Honor the specialness of the times spent together. Make a playhouse out of a refrigerator box, roast marshmallows in the backyard on a star-filled night or sing them a special birthday song you wrote. In years to come, your children probably will count these as some of their favorite memories.

When our eldest daughter, Shayna, was only five, someone brought her a very expensive sophisticated electronic toy. It walked, talked, flashed lights and responded to voice commands. Shayna played with it delightedly for about 45 minutes until, because of its complex but poor design, it broke irreparably.

Deep into her tears of frustration, Shayna stopped crying when she saw her dad cutting holes into the large cardboard carton the toy had come in.

"Look, Shayna, here's how we can make this into a spaceship!" Hanoch said.

He hunkered down on the floor and included her in the game. He had crayons, markers, tape and scissors. Sitting on the living room carpet, the two of them decorated the new spaceship and happily flew it around the universe. Tears forgotten, Shayna discovered the wonders of cardboard cartons plus imagination.

Years later, Shayna — who is now about to be married — still remembers the magic spaceship. But the memory of the expensive toy that broke faded.

Even the most mundane parts of our experience can be made special with the magic power that all parents possess in a child's eyes. Through your children's joy, you will rediscover the exuberance of innocent youth.

A Note To The Wiser

Despite the advent of labor-saving gadgets and high-tech devices designed to make our existence easier, our lives seem to get away from us.

"I don't have time for that," we say plaintively.

The late Harry Chapin wrote a poignant song, "Cat's Cradle," that paints a picture of a father who was always just a bit too busy to spend time with his son. The haunting refrain says, "When're you coming home, Dad?"

"I don't know when, but we'll get together then, Son, we'll get together then."

With each verse, the boy gets older, but the Dad's busyness continues and the times they want to share are postponed again.

Suddenly, the son is grown and moved away. The father, now retired, asks, "When're you coming over, Son?" You can guess his son's answer. His son, after all, wanted to grow up just like Dad.

Contrast that with the story of a well-respected newspaperman at the Seattle bureau of the Associated Press. Patrick Connolly left for work before his kids got up and, like many fathers, often returned home long after they'd gone to bed.

One way he shared his love, values, and talents with his boys was to share his thoughts through notes, including his talent for cartooning and humor.

Connolly compiled hundreds of these notes, cartoons, bits of wisdom, and love into a book for his boys called *Love, Dad.* An untimely heart attack at age 42 took Connolly from his family, but they had this wonderful legacy with which to remember him.

Sometimes our lives are too full of things that have to get done. But time is a precious commodity. Perhaps Pat Connolly's answer is a good one for us: write. Write something. It doesn't have to be a great work of literature, just something from your heart. It may become a family treasure.

Here are some additional ways to express your love to your family through writing:

- Put a note in your child's lunch box: "You did a beautiful job cleaning up the kitchen last night, honey, I appreciate you"; or "Thanks for making such an effort in school. Your report card tells me you're right on track."
- On the weekly grocery list circle the ingredients of a favorite dish and write, "I love this special meal and the love you put into making it."
- Gary Larson, author of *The Far Side* cartoon, publishes a daily cartoon calendar. Recycle the cartoons by cutting off the date and writing a love note or affirmation on them. That is recycling with a heart!

- If you do the laundry for your family tuck love notes in among their folded clothes .
- Sneak a love note in her luggage so that your loved one gets a warm, loved feeling from home on the trip. It might even help her sleep better.
- Make up a simple love song with your own words to an old tune. For example, to the tune of "Row, Row, Row Your Boat," compose a little personalized ditty like this:

  "I love Mac so much, he's really fun to hug.
  Merrily, merrily, merrily, he's my little bug."
- Learn the sign language for "I love you."
- Write "I love you" on a loved one's hands.
- Mail letters or cards to your kids or spouse even if they haven't gone away. It's fun to get mail for any reason or no reason at all.
- Write a love note on a helium balloon and hide it in an unexpected place, such as the closet, pantry, bathroom or workbench.
- If you have a home computer, use the *Print Shop* or *Bannermania* software programs to create your own "Welcome Home" or "Congratulations" signs.
- Cut a heart out of cardboard. Write "I love you" on it, cut it into puzzle pieces and leave it in an envelope for the one you adore to find and put together.
- Make a love collage. Our eldest daughter made a long collage with art work, pictures of us, shells and silly sayings for our wedding present. To us, it's worth its weight in gold.

- Write a silly "knock, knock" joke:
  "Knock, Knock!"
  "Who's there?"
  "Olive."
  "Olive, who?"
  "Olive you!"
- Say "I love you" in different languages:
  French: Je t'aime.
  Spanish: Te amo.
  German: Ich liebe dich.
  Italian: Lo tiamo.
- Fill a pretty jar with nuts, circle it with a ribbon and attach a note that says, "Call me crazy, but I'm nuts about you."

Value what you do and do what you value.
— Values Realization Institute

Your ulcers can't grow while you're laughing.
— Hunter Adams M.D.

Learning From The Masters

We once had a discussion with our friend, Eric, about acts of kindness in relationships. He felt the key to keeping a relationship alive was to perform loving acts on a regular basis.

"I never miss a chance to send flowers," he said. "I can't believe guys don't catch on to this quicker in their married lives."

A survey was taken recently of couples who've been married 25 years or longer. When asked what their secret is for a long and happy marriage, the standard response was "working at love every day."

Do you read the classics, observe and appreciate fine art and listen to good music from famous musicians? Writers, artists and musicians try to emulate the masters in their fields. In the art form of love, learn and copy the acts of loving kindness from the masters — the couples who have made their marriages work over a long period of time. Make a date to study the relationship strategies from those couples who make love-giving and receiving a daily routine. It might spark creativity and enthusiasm in your love relationship.

Being Fully Present

People make demands on our time every day, from our children to our bosses to our spouses. Not being able to meet these demands is frustrating. Making time for ourselves often is impossible. Crowded schedules can mean that our minds are not able to focus on any one thing.

I had come home tired from a busy day at work. I began fixing dinner, put in a load of laundry and helped our son with his science lesson. I turned on the phone recorder and listened to the message while putting the old newspapers in the recycling bin. Our daughter excitedly followed me around, telling me about something that happened at school. I was only half-listening, desperately tired and anxious that I wouldn't have the strength to get through all the household chores before my energy ran out.

Finally, I'd had enough chattering. I was annoyed that she was pestering me when I had so much to accomplish. I stopped dead in my tracks with the intent of yelling, "Mommy is busy! Just let me get through dinner and then I'll deal with whatever's going on with you."

Yelling would have been easy, but it would have made me feel even worse and would have burned my daughter in the process.

Instead, I took a deep breath, let it out very slowly and said, "I'd like to make a date with you after dinner when we can both talk and listen to one another without all the noise and confusion of our family chores. I'll meet you at the big blue chair at 7:00 P.M. Please help me out with the dinner so I can be ready in time to relax and really enjoy what you have to say."

I got the extra help and my daughter got my full attention.

A simple act of kindness is being fully present for another person. It shows that you're giving all of yourself because the other person deserves it. It models for them their value to you and allows you to expect the same from them. The bond between you will be strengthened because of your attentiveness.

The next time you have the opportunity, be fully present for someone you care about. Be a good listener, make eye contact, listen as though this is the most important information you've ever heard and resist the temptation to interrupt. Smile and nod in agreement if it's appropriate and cherish the moment. It's one of life's healthier pleasures.

Time, time, time, I wish I had more time!
— *Everybody*

That Picture-Perfect Moment

Have you ever run into the problem of what to give Grandma and Grandpa for a special holiday or birthday? They seem to have everything and a new blender just isn't personal or special enough. When you reach a certain age, you understand the value of memories versus "things."

If your extended family is far away, it's easy to let special events slip by and not remember them. One way that I've found to include people in a big way is the photo calendar. It's a big hit, not only with Grandma and Grandpa, but the whole family. (See the Resources section for ordering information).

Capture that special moment by carrying your camera with you to as many events as possible. The candid and playful shots are the most fun.

Send in the photo and a short caption and within a few weeks you'll receive the finished product (and your original).

Acts Of Kindness In The Workplace

Service With A Smile

If you own a business, outstanding service is an act of kindness you must always give your customers. Good service is not a fad, it's always in style. Paying attention to lavish details, listening to customers and investing in employee motivation brings people back to you because they feel good.

Stay as close to your customers as possible. Service-with-care works for everyone. It costs five times as much to gain a new customer as it does to keep a current one. Studies show that 91 percent of unhappy customers will never purchase goods or services from you again. If you make an effort to remedy buyer complaints, 82 percent to 95 percent of your customers will stay with you.

Simply listen and respond to your customers as often as possible. The customer needs satisfaction, but keeps coming back to you because your concern has a positive emotional effect on him.

Kindness Counts: The Seven Secrets Of Success

1. Hire people who like people. Train them and treat them well.
2. Have customers define kindness and have your employees provide it. Meet with your customers and

ask them what they feel needs to happen for them to get good service. Raise your employees' awareness level to meet the new kindness standards.

3. Attitude is everything. Hire folks who are kind and receptive to the service culture you're trying to create. When interviewing them ask how they would react to some typical customer situations.
4. Train without strain. Invest in the caring concern of your employees by increasing their abilities to solve customer problems on their own. It will empower them and build loyalty to an organization that considers their professional growth.
5. Give employees stipends for saving the company money or institute a profit-sharing program. Incentive programs create an impetus for success.
6. Walk the walk and talk the talk. Give employees the latitude and power to make decisions that result in bottom-line customer satisfaction.
7. Recognize, affirm and validate your employees continually.

Listen, Understand, Respond

There is no perfect way to listen to your customers. The caring employee acts as if there is always more to learn. Here are some tips for better customer service:

- Show that you care about your customers. Ask, "What do you like about doing business with our company? Are we dependable? If not, where do you feel we can improve?"
- Do a perception check. Send your employees out for a professional growth day to gain insight from your competitors and bring back ideas about how they are caring for their customers.
- Establish a "customer kindness hotline" with a toll-free number. Keep in touch with customer concerns.
- Establish a "customer kindness advisory panel" to meet with customers regularly and provide compensation.

You Can Never Do Too Much — More Customer Service Tips

- Remember names.
- Keep facilities sparkling clean.
- Put out fresh flowers.
- Invest in an attractive environment.
- Strive for speed and accuracy.
- Be honest about equipment breakdowns.
- Give customers a genuine smile.
- When challenged about a problem, don't argue — apologize and make amends.

You Can Never Do Too Much, Or Can You?

Some companies differ on this philosophy. They believe in the so-called "80/20 rule" which says that, "80% of your time is spent dealing with 20 percent of your customers," or, "80 percent of your company's profits come from 20 percent of your customers." Whatever the version, the basic idea is to focus your efforts on the most profitable customers.

As we write this, two giant Fortune 500 companies announced they're laying off thousands of workers. The first, to save the company, as a result of either: (a) poor world-wide economic conditions and the predations of Japanese competitors or, (b) incredibly poor management.

In either case, about 86,000 workers will come home without jobs. The bottom line is the deciding factor: the company will shut down if employees are not laid off.

The second company is laying off 13,000 workers to be more profitable. Despite earning record profits — generated by these same 13,000 folks about to get the ax — the wise leaders of this company want to make even more profits, so they are "right-sizing," a euphemism used to justify firing everyone except the people using the term! "We're going to be lean and mean." Yes, mean is right.

What becomes of those 13,000 people? Will they have the money to buy the products of their erstwhile company? Even more interesting, what happens to the motivation and esprit de corps of the workers left behind? Will they be loyal, creative or committed to increasing the company's competitiveness? Our guess is they'll be motivated by fear, running scared, stressed out, impatient, fiercely competitive, and either lackadaisical or conspiratorial. Everyone, including the customer, loses.

Fax Of Kindness

The fax is a recent medium of communicaton that can be raised to a new and warmer level by adding:

- A warm personal note to build a relationship.
- Some humor —

  Choose an unusual typeface to express an idea.

  Add an appropriate joke or funny quote.

  Include a cartoon that makes your point.

  Take a photo of a famous person from the newspaper, add a word-balloon and a caption that gets your point across.
- An apology, when necessary, written by hand to make it warmer and more genuine.
- A validation of the other person, department or company using words like respect, valued for, appreciate, cherish, delighted by, can count on you, etc.
- Your company's mission statement to communicate its values.
- An affirming, positive or inspiring article you recently read or wrote.

Principles Of Kinder Faxing

- Make them short; save the recipient time and save some trees, too!
- Make them very, very clear.
- Make sure they are honest, authentic and represent you and your company well. Never fire off an angry fax. Let the angry ones sit for several days until your anger is cooled. Then re-read and reconsider.
- When possible, they should be encouraging and positive. Don't use a fax to slam the door.
- Make them warm. Express feelings, not just facts.
- Add some humor. Save a file of funny quotes and cartoons which are relevant issues in your industry and use them for fax cover pages.

A Positive Conspiracy

Supervising employees is a big responsibility. How you handle power, cope with stress and express your values and humanity affect the workplace tremendously. All too often, a supervisor is the subject of the "ain't-it-awful" staff gossip. If there's a breach of trust and negative criticism coming from the supervisor, there is a way to break the cycle and remedy things with an act-of-kindness-conspiracy.

Begin by brainstorming with the group about what unmet needs they think the supervisor has which may be creating such a flow of anger, criticism or blame. Then conspire to do five or six things that help to meet those needs. When people's legitimate needs are met, they are much more likely to be pleasant, caring and trustworthy.

People who have performed this act of kindness recount a transformation in the person they targeted with kindness. Remove the titles and status and we're all just people who appreciate kindness.

Kindly Clowning

Stress in the workplace can take its toll on our mental and physical well-being. If the workload can't be decreased, humor and kindness can come to the rescue.

Ten Playful Ways To Use Humor And Kindness To Lighten The Work Load:

1. When you're kept on hold too long, remember you are always free to hang up. If it's very important to stay on the line, think about how little help you'll get if you explode when the person returns. Instead of getting mad, share a funny cartoon, a gentle joke or a pleasant remark about the day with the human being on the other end of the line. Remember Mom and Dad's first lesson, "Sharing is good."
2. Put a mirror on your desk and draw in a funny face to superimpose on yours. When you're dealing with difficult people, look in the mirror. The chuckle you get will give you the gift of perspective and the delight of secret laughter. When we're being attacked or criticized we give over our own sense of power to the other person by becoming defensive. Be kind to yourself by examining what is true about what the speaker said, and let go of what is not.

3. Make your point with cartoons. Adding cartoons to agendas and memos helps to drive your point home, even if it is a sensitive issue.
4. Put on your funny glasses to help you look for the obvious humor waiting to be discovered. Make it a point to look for opportunities to use humor to help your colleagues put the incongruities of life in perspective.

   Perfection is something we're all pretty uptight about. Recognize, and laugh hard and long when you make a silly mistake. The kindness is in granting your own imperfections and giving others permission to laugh with you. Just don't use humor to avoid accepting blame for a big mistake.
5. Add something humorous to the agenda of your office meeting.
6. Serve lollipops or ice cream at your next meeting. Communication is improved because these snacks lighten the atmosphere and besides, it's also very difficult to argue with someone who is trying desperately to lick a dripping cone.
7. Have a party funded by bad habits. Get the most ridiculous looking container you can find and require that swearing, complaining, gossiping people contribute to the party fund. Every four months, use the money for a staff get-together.
8. When you've done something you're really proud

of, give yourself a big hand or "ta da!" If no one will give you a standing ovation, give yourself one. Establish a rule in your work-group that anyone who finishes a big task well really will get a standing ovation. We've been doing this one for years. It's a surefire winner.

9. Give out monthly awards for the most creative use of telephone time, late-to-work excuses and expense account rationalizations.
10. Add "finding humor" to your "to do" list. When you have found something humorous, mark it off your list and jot down what you have found.

Take your job seriously and yourself lightly.
— *Joel Goodman*

Messages That Mean Welcome

Have you ever looked forward to going to certain business establishments? Even if your business there isn't particularly rewarding you come away feeling cared about. The Galt, California, post office in my community is one of those places.

The post office is unique because it has Peggy, who appears to do a little of everything except deliver mail. It's the caring way she does everything that makes the difference! Her style of greeting and taking care of her friends and customers is so inviting. Actually I walk out of the post office feeling better than when I came in.

Here are eight reasons why Peggy's customers always feel welcome:

1. She calls everyone by name, remembers their names and if she doesn't know them, she asks.
2. She greets all with a smile, makes direct eye contact, and asks how they are.
3. She works extremely fast, which is considerate of customers' time.
4. She gives customers worthwhile information.
5. She gives a credible and warm face to the U.S. Postal Service.

6. She is quick to laugh and be playful including keeping a humorous quote for the day on the counter.
7. Often she greets folks with a handshake.
8. She's extraordinarily helpful. She once helped an aging customer rewrap her package because the lady didn't have the strength to do so properly herself. Peggy found some packing material and patiently helped this lady. She got another counter person to help with the line so no one was inconvenienced. Everyone in line smiled and several murmured words of appreciation while they watched her with this customer.

May I Have This Dance?

Small tokens of kindness bond peers, creating team mentality. Acts of kindness fill in the gaps when the doldrums overtake us or our creativity isn't as accessible as we'd like.

Here are some team-building acts of kindness:

- Search for cartoons that capture the essence of a particularly difficult issue at your workplace. Humor frees creativity and could unblock the solution to the problem.
- Find a particular characteristic unique to individual coworkers and celebrate them for it throughout the work year. A friend shared with us a story about an employer who knew his secretary loved to dance. One special birthday, as she entered the office, he presented her with a corsage, turned on a cassette of her favorite music, bowed and asked, "May I have this dance?" After the dance was over, he thanked her, wished her a happy birthday, and went back to his normal work routine. The long-lasting effect of the act left her feeling cherished, appreciated and celebrated.

- Dr. Michele Borba shares many wonderful ways of keeping kindness on a roll at work. One we particularly like is using food puns. For example, put an orange on a new employee's desk with a note that says, "Orange you glad you came to work here? We are! Welcome aboard." Another good one is to place a Payday candy bar in someone's mailbox with a note that reads, "You don't have to wait until payday to be appreciated around here. I appreciate the contribution you make!" Be creative! The possibilities are endless.
- Bring in a "friendship cake" and share it. Organize a friendship lunch and have everyone bring their favorite food to share. Use the friendship cake for dessert.
- Dr. Bernie Siegal has a sign in his office that reads, "If you're ever less than a B, tell us and we'll hug you."
- Make a commitment to safety. If working late, walk out to the parking lot in groups. Be conscious of any strangers in the work environment. Be aware of leaving equipment/materials on the floor that may be a physical hazard to mobility. The kindness-minded employee cares for self and others.
- Keeping confidentiality is a challenge in the workplace that can make or break employee relations. If a colleague discusses a personal issue with you, keep it confidential.

Check for Understanding

Diversity in the workplace is both a strength and a weakness. When you bring a variety of individuals with different value systems, ethnicity's and communication styles into a work setting, it can stimulate creative problem solving. It can also be a breeding ground for disagreements and misunderstandings. Clearing the air can take a lot of energy and tenacity, but there are some caring ways to model communication skills that allow everyone to be heard and respected:

- Check for understanding: If you are at all unsure of the meaning or intention of the speaker, repeat back for her what you understood her to say: "What I heard you say was . . ."
- Rephrase: This act of kindness doesn't put a value on what was said or make a judgment of right or wrong, it just allows you to put what was said into your own words. The speaker, for example, says, "I saw the masked man walk behind me into the bank and I thought it was the end of me." The listener who rephrases says, "So you were pretty excited when you saw a masked man behind you and probably feared for your life."

- Tell me more: This phrase invites the speaker to elaborate on her concerns or excitement. It is also an endearing phrase that sends the message to the speaker that you value what she has to say.

  Other key phrases:

  Tell me more about . . .
  Help me understand . . .
  How did you come to feel that way?
  What sense do you make of that?
  How do you interpret that?
  What does that mean to you?
  How does that make you feel?
  What does that make you want to do?
  How can we go on from here?

- The I-message: This is the act of owning responsibility for your feelings about the subject without stating blame. For example: "I get anxious in a situation like this because I feel I'm being taken advantage of."

- Validate and affirm: Thank the other person for expressing his feelings even if you don't agree with him. Everyone has a right to her or his own feelings. If you bury feelings, you bury them alive and they will resurface in different ways. Appreciation helps to build bridges between people and allows them to reconnect.

- Add levity to the gravity of the situation: If you have a disagreement, look for something absurd in the situation to help lighten the atmosphere. This diffuses the anger, or fear that extends a disagreement. The use of humor is a mature coping tool as long as it isn't negative or sarcastic humor. Use humor to lighten and amuse, not to abuse.

As a word of warning, be careful about the use of humor when people are angry. There is always the chance that you will be seen as trivializing or minimizing the other's feelings or patronizing them. Humor should not be used as a distraction to avoid solving a problem. The point of using humor is to release the tension and allow all parties to see each other just as people. When you do get back to dealing with the problem, you'll usually be seen as being helpful and kind.

Humor is like a needle and thread,
deftly used it can patch up just about anything.
— Unknown

When I ignore my feelings,
my stomach keeps score.
— Anon

Booster Shot

Everyone in the office needs a little boost once in awhile. A bit of recognition can get creative juices flowing again and can also reduce stress.

People need to be validated and they also need to connect with others at work. One way to connect or reconnect personnel is to start with the office bulletin board. Call it the Positive Information Center. It can be a real booster shot for morale.

Here are three ideas to get you started:

1. Somebody's Baby: Have everyone bring a favorite baby or early childhood picture to the office for the bulletin board. People should include a quote with their picture regarding something funny about how they viewed the world as a child, or what they wanted to do when they grew up.

   A variation of this is to have everyone bring in a baby picture (without showing them to anyone). One person gets them all, mixes them up numbers and posts them on a bulletin board. Each employee in the office gets an answer sheet and the winner is the one who can correctly identify every baby!

2. Humor Board: Initiate your own office humor bulletin board. The criteria for the board is to have positive humor that does not use prejudice, negative criticism or sarcasm to hurt a coworker. This is a place to list ways to look at things with a humorous perspective.
3. Picture This: Get a photograph of everyone in your office wearing costumes — perhaps from last year's Halloween party. Post the picture and a sign that reads, "Would you work with these people?"

Adding Appreciation To The Workplace

The workplace is a community that needs constant tending to its human needs as well as its business needs. Building connectedness and appreciation is an ongoing process. Work is not just about succeeding in a business, it's about caring for your customers and your colleagues. When we work toward getting the job done in an empowering, creative, exciting and caring manner, success is guaranteed.

Using affirmations and validations to show appreciation and encouragement are two of the most powerful, long-lasting strategies a business can use. Notes left anywhere in the office will be relished.

Sidney Simon has a recipe for affirmations that will help to jumpstart your imagination and creativity. He reminds us that the criteria for a good affirmation is that it must be genuine, short and clear.

Some of Simon's affirmation starters are:

I thank you for . . .
I value you for . . .
I celebrate you for . . .
I respect you for . . .
I admire the way that you . . .
I was pleased when you . . .

A playful way we've used the affirmation notes in the workplace has been associated with holidays. We've gathered affirmations for each employee from the management, peers and staff and stuffed them and a lottery ticket in colorful plastic Easter eggs, or a box of Matzoh for Passover. The staff really values these acts of appreciation and looks forward to them yearly.

Another way to use affirmations is to print them on a notepad and have them readily available so that even in a meeting, when you hear something positive you can "catch people in the act of doing it right." Or make a poster of affirmation sentence stems and put it up prominently in your meeting room.

Acts Of Kindness That Rebuild And Renew

Even The Score

How do you bring hope to what appears to be a hopeless situation? If you could bring even one small ray of hope, wouldn't that be a spectacular act of kindness?

Consider Faye Rumphs, who received a call from the police that her son had been murdered senselessly in a drive-by shooting, probably a victim of a gang with initiation rites requiring the death of innocent victims.

In a similar situation, would you retaliate? Rumphs' way of dealing with the grief and injustice was to commit herself to making a difference in stopping the cycle.

"I decided I wasn't going to accept my son's death and do nothing. I wanted to keep kids out of gangs and the best way to do that was to keep them busy," said Rumphs.

In honor of her son, who despised gangs, Faye created the Al Wooten, Jr. Heritage Center, an after-school learning refuge for about two dozen kids, ages 7 to 18.

The center offers supplemental courses six days per week for kids enrolled in the school system. College students and professionals volunteer their time in a mix of classes such as black history, spelling, entrepreneurship and learning to learn. The school, in the heart of riot-scarred South Central L.A., is a godsend to many.

Rumphs brought kids in off the streets of poverty and despair and provided a safe haven in which to learn and grow. It doesn't really matter that the school's not accredited, what *does* matter is that a courageous person with a grieving but healing heart puts herself on the line for kids.

The goals of the center are to: get the kids to understand that life is worth living in a proper way; help them to become aware that there are people who care about them; keep them from dropping out; and get them off the streets by providing them with a safe, empowering haven.

Faye sold her home to fund the center and since that time has operated on a scant budget of $18,000 per year with revenue from grants, fund-raisers and donations.

When rioting broke out over the Rodney King verdict in 1992, Rumphs' kids were not among the looters.

"I told them, the way to change future verdicts is to get an education and vote," said Rumphs

The kids used that negative energy and turned it into something positive by not looting and by helping with the clean-up efforts, including that of a ransacked Korean grocery store.

When asked about her center, Rumphs says, "It's about children."

Having lost her own child, she's gained many through her acts of hope and kindness.

Voice-Mail Technology That Empowers The Homeless

Homeless, but not hopeless is the motto of the Community Worker's Center in Seattle, Washington, which has created a personal message center for the homeless using telephone voice mail.

Homeless job-seekers often are unable to find steady employment — even though they are able-bodied and have useful skills — because they don't have a phone. They remain stuck in a vicious cycle: without steady employment, they remain homeless; without a home, they can't find steady employment.

The center's act of kindness helps people help themselves. Since it opened, 126 people have found jobs through the program and 70 people have found housing.

The non-profit center operates the voice mail with donations and the support of the Active Voice Corporation.

See the Resources section for more information regarding the project.

Shopping For Self-Esteem

Directly in back of Carter G. Woodson Jr. High School in Washington, D.C., the country's youngest entrepreneurs have opened shop at the Conner-Harris II Mini Mall.

Named for two local students who lost their lives in drug disputes, the mall was founded in 1988 by former police officer W.W. Johnson, who was weary and discouraged from "seeing young people killed every night."

Running a retail operation has given Woodson students a working knowledge of real businessworld concepts: credit, overhead, profits, losses and investments.

"But more important," said Johnson, "they learn something money can't buy — self-esteem."

Johnson understood that more force was not the answer. In 1989, he was transferred to the position of public safety officer at a local school. He modeled positive action by organizing the refurbishment of a burnt-out classroom which he turned into a weight-lifting room. The kids needed a safe, fun and empowering place to hang out and learn. Johnson's act of kindness was to send the messages that there is a better life and that kids can also be agents for change.

Acts That Build Bridges Over Barriers Between Cultures

Many barriers exist to meaningful cross-cultural understanding. Not wanting to stand out, people from other cultures may retreat and say little, which prevents them from fitting in and connecting. They are often lonely and confused.

One way to bridge the gap between cultures is through education. Amherst Regional High School in Amherst, Massachusetts, developed a culture-to-culture project that brought students together to learn about each other and their cultures.

This project provided time for students to interview one another, discuss friendships, hopes and first experiences in the United States. The interviews were videotaped and shown to other young people in the hope of bridging some of the gaps of confusion.

If you would like to help someone from another culture adapt to the American melting pot, here are some ideas for bridging the gap:

- Speak as clearly as possible. If you don't think the person understood what you said, rephrase it.

- If he communicates to you and you are not sure of his intent, rephrase it for him and ask if that is what he meant.
- Ask lots of questions. Show interest.
- Avoid stereotypes.
- Watch for newcomers to include in your activities. Convey that newcomers are welcomed and encouraged.
- Keep the inclusion techniques coming. Often quietness is rewarded by being ignored. Support people need to be aware of this.
- Humor is universal. Some of the nuances of the English language can be a challenge and you may need to explain the humor when first attempting it. Explaining a joke or funny circumstance can water-down the humor, but persist anyway. There are great connections between human beings that will work even if other techniques fail.
- Create a social gathering and invite everyone to bring the special food of their culture. There is comfort and pleasure in favorite foods that bring memories of good times. Ask guests to bring copies of their recipe. You'll find that many cultural recipes have ingredients in common.
- Do the "thumbs up" activity with folks. In this activity you ask people to clasp their hands with their fingers

naturally interwoven. Ask them to be aware of which thumb they have on top of the other (right or left). Ask them to clasp their hands again but with the opposite thumb on top. Ask them how it feels. Most folks will report that it feels uncomfortable or unnatural. Ask them if either is right or wrong. Invite them to consider the idea that there is no right or wrong culture, just many likenesses and differences. Have them list likenesses and differences. This can be a real eye-opener for those people who are visual learners.

- Ask folks to share their music, art, story-telling and goals. By making the effort to bridge the barriers between cultures, you receive the gift of knowing many wonderful people with unique experiences, and you give the gift of building and rebuilding a more understanding and tolerant world. In fact, we'd like to move past mere tolerance to help people reach a state of appreciation.

How Can We Understand Those We Do Not Know?

Many people were surprised and horrified when violence erupted across the country in response to the not-guilty verdicts in the trial of four Los Angeles police officers accused of beating Rodney King. Why were we shocked? Perhaps because we do not understand the feelings and responses of those involved.

Few people condone violence as a response to any disappointing event, yet we can't pretend it didn't happen. It affected all of us and will for a long time, and we all have certain responsibilities as a result.

Sensitivity 101

When I first worked with children who had been abused and molested, I did not understand their self-destructive behavior. It shocked and saddened me. Because I did not understand them, I was unable to support them.

As I learned more and talked to the children about their feelings and reactions to stress, I increased my awareness level enough to be able to help them break their penchant for self-destructive actions.

I think that the same can be done in response to the violence and destruction that occurred and is still occurring.

Bring up your awareness level and be part of change. The problem won't just go away.

To be a part of this force for change, try practicing some of these sensitivity acts:

- Gain knowledge of other people's circumstances. Begin by talking to folks who are involved.
- Help with the clean-up process by finding out what the people who are in the situation say they need.
- Present your findings to the closest think tank. Put the challenge to our future leaders: the student councils and student governments of our schools.
- Become aware of what is age-appropriate behavior and behavior typical to various cultural, ethnic and religious groups. Judging another group by your own standards breeds misunderstanding.
- Commit to know the people you deal with. It's easy to hate faceless and anonymous people. Find out about them.
- Try walking a mile in someone else's shoes and learn to understand the behavior you see, not just the media's view.
- Extend your global awareness and sensitivity to anyone discriminated against, oppressed or devalued.

Acts Of Kindness To The Homeless

Out of the corner of our eye we see them huddled under highway overpasses, begging on street corners and sleeping on park benches. They are the homeless, whose tragic plight tugs at our heart, but generally not enough to take action to help them.

Who are the homeless? According to research, the population is divided. Some are mental patients who were forced out on the street when funding sources dried-up and patients' rights were defined as not keeping patients against their will. Others are hoboes or addicts. There are single mothers who have been divorced, fled abusive spouses, and can't pay for housing. These people are on the street because the human community was not able or willing to support them as needed.

If the issue of homelessness is of real concern to you, there are some things you can do to make a difference. We believe there is a bundle of "kindness energy" in all of us that can come out, given a focus or a strategy for doing so. If some of the suggestions do not feel comfortable to you, read on, there are many ideas in a small or large scale from which to choose.

- Get to know one homeless person. You can find them in shelters, soup kitchens, public health clinics, park benches, libraries and bus stations. Don't have a set agenda other than just getting to know him. Be honest in your discussion with him. Tell him you are concerned about the plight of the homeless and that you want to know an actual person so you can learn more about how to be part of making a positive change in the world. Don't apologize for having more than he does, just share yourself as one person to another. Don't promise to return if you won't. Keep a record of what you learned and who you talked to, your feelings and impressions.
- Recognize them. The homeless know they are invisible to us. Give them the gift of knowing somebody realizes they exist. Share with them a smile, eye contact, a laugh or an experience. It is so painful to be so totally invisible, many homeless report.
- Simply listen to them. Avoid the urge to blame them for their situation or label them as victims. Such talk is dehumanizing.
- Look for their strengths and their talents. Reinforce them when they speak of options. Stand in line with folks on the street. You don't need to dress up or down or be extremely jovial. As you spend time in the line it will help you become aware of the forces and

choices that put folks on the street. Be authentic with them and absorb and enjoy their stories.

- If you have a talent for problem-solving, help them learn the skills to do so themselves. Not everyone is good at making choices and would do better if they knew how. Practice your own understanding of their condition, then teach skills. Refrain from trying to solve their problems.
- Help your friend open a bank account so that his money will be safe. Help him with strategies for money management and be understanding and persistent with him when mistakes challenge his skills.
- Educate yourself about the Aid to Families with Dependent Children program (AFDC). Call your local welfare office and ask them about the amount of money a typical family receives, how food stamps are used and provisions for rent, medical and child-care assistance.
- Volunteer in a soup kitchen. If the thought frightens you, ask a friend to go with you.
- Visit a homeless person in jail. Don't assume you have answers before you get there, just ask about her story. The act of kindness is to listen and learn.
- Volunteer in a day-shelter for children. Learn and build trust.
- Attend a city council meeting when an agenda pertaining to homelessness is being discussed. Speak of

your experience with the homeless, be authentic and state the facts.

- Encourage and validate those police officers who support the homeless.
- Build a house for the homeless. There are organizations that do just that. The best known is Habitat for Humanity — in the directory in most cities under Habitat. You can contribute money to them directly and their group of volunteers will use the money to build houses. Another option is to have your club or organization take on a construction project with their support. This is a good investment of your time and money.
- Persuade your church congregation or organization to offer a day shelter for women and children. Work within your community to provide regular, low-cost day-care for poor, working mothers with homes. Some families are only one or two house payments away from being on the streets. If you support the opportunities for them to keep working, they can continue to have a roof over their heads.
- Make a gift of a public transportation pass to a homeless friend. Most cities provide a weekly pass for about $10. This can provide the opportunity for the family provider to get to and from work until she gets her feet on steady ground.

- If your community or county has a task force for the homeless, join it, learn from it and see what you can do to help. We have joined the Sacramento County Task Force for Homeless Children and it has been a real learning experience. We discovered the very special problems of homeless kids. Can you imagine never getting to go to school, or going to a different school every six to eight weeks as your parents wander from county to county seeking benefits? (County welfare benefits in many locations expire cyclically.)
- Talk with distributors of children's clothing and ask them if they would be willing to donate seconds to the local clothes closet. Research indicates that homeless students want to attend school, and will, if they are not embarrassed by their clothing.
- Some dry cleaners will clean jackets and coats and distribute them to Goodwill or other social service agencies. If you have a coat or jacket you no longer need or care to wear, it might be of great comfort to someone in need of warmth.

Kindness For Hard Times

Economic downturns affect all of us. Many talented, hard-working folks were laid off unexpectedly and now wait in growing lines at state unemployment offices. Those with a diploma and a supportive family network at least have a chance of staying afloat. Others without these resources have a much more difficult time.

There are many ways that you can provide kind acts of support for those facing hard times. Here are just a few:

- Refrain from saying, "A person can always find a job and support his family if he really wants to." Some folks are only a circumstance away from the street, without the shelter of health insurance, an education or a family support network.
- If you know of a person with heavy responsibilities facing a layoff — a baby on the way or an invalid parent they care for — help her write a letter to her employer to extend their health care coverage until she can get back on her feet. Also, become familiar with the Consolidated Omnibus Budget Reconciliation Act of 1985 (COBRA) regulations regarding health-care coverage and make sure she understands them. Assist the person by contacting the media regarding

her plight. Someone out there might need just the talents this person has to offer.

- Many folks are among the ranks of the working poor. They have jobs but don't make enough to pay for housing. You can help. Write a letter to the Department of Housing and Urban Development (HUD) and ask what is being done in your area to provide available and affordable housing. Ask what you can do to help.

Getting Back On the Right Track

The Voluntary Action Center (VAC), a service of the Community United Way of Pioneer Valley, Massachusetts, matches volunteers with the needs in the community.

The center operates Horizons, a shelter for homeless mothers and pregnant women from 16 to 24 years old. The program accepts six fortunate women who receive shelter, specialized educational workshops, skill training and vocational guidance.

Volunteers Make The Difference

The program works because of its volunteers. They are women who have been through similar life experiences and succeeded. They help residents learn how to manage a budget, communicate effectively, provide their families with inexpensive and nutritious meals, deal with children's behavior and other essential living skills. They are kindness models.

Volunteers are also part of the peer-support system in rebuilding community connections. They are isolation-breakers and loneliness-busters. The relationships they develop continue after the resident leaves the shelter. They are friends, spend time together, and share experiences.

Volunteers work anywhere from two to eight hours per week. They are of all ages and provide strong shoulders to cry on and arms to hug with when celebrating each step of success.

Sometimes they assist in reuniting families. This helps not only the people involved, but the community at large, since social service programs are so costly to maintain.

If you would like to volunteer to help women and children in your community, here are some acts of kindness that you can provide:

- Solicit donations to keep a program like Horizons alive in the face of declining municipal budgets.
- Hold a fundraising event to benefit the center.
- Work with the community to convert unused property or shelters into affordable housing.
- Teach or share your skills of household care and maintenance, budget management and behavior management.
- If you have a special talent, volunteer to work with children who have physical or emotional challenges. This is a great need.
- Become a tutor.

For information about the Voluntary Action Center, please see the Resources section.

Trading Services For Groceries

Some people do not have enough to eat and don't feel like a valuable part of the community. A program called Share U.S.A. helps fulfill both these needs. It is designed to help people stretch their food dollars while giving them an opportunity to use their talents to make their community a safer, happier and more loving place.

The program, first started in California, offers people $30 to 35-worth of nutritious food every month in exchange for $14 and two hours of community service. Donated services can include baby-sitting, giving a disabled person a ride to a doctor's appointment or volunteering in a shelter or school.

Not only do these people receive food, but the program attaches meaning to their work. This empowers them to break the cycle of dependency and changes their view of their own value to society as independent, functional people. It feeds the body and soul.

When crisis hits, it's often very difficult for people to refocus their thinking. It's a challenge for them to go from a drowning person to being their own life preserver. They have a difficult time recognizing personal talents and attributes that are valuable to other people — who may also be drowning. Another valuable trait of this program is that it reconnects people who may otherwise have isolated themselves because of their circumstances.

The volunteer action helps to rebuild the community at the grass-roots level. A perception shift occurs because when people invest their time and talent, they gain a sense of personal control and community spirit. It is a necessary and novel way to deal with local-level budget cuts, and getting things done that local funds can no longer support.

Share USA can be found in most major cities. Three that we are aware of are located in San Francisco, San Diego and Springfield, Massachusetts.

Rebuilding: Random Acts Of Kindness Versus Random Acts Of Violence

The nightly news is filled with stories of cities torn apart by random violence. The world, it seems, is spinning out of control with thugs taking over our streets and poverty, drug abuse and despair claiming people's lives. But there is hope. There is a movement growing throughout the country and it's looking for a few good movers and shakers: "goodness guerrillas" fighting for human kindness. This movement has really always been around on an individual basis, but it is beginning to catch on as more and more people want to make a difference.

One of the goodness guerrillas is Anne Herbert, a Mill Valley, California, writer who coined the credo, "Practice random kindness and senseless acts of beauty." Her followers have inscribed this phrase on highway underpasses, bumpers stickers, placemats in restaurants and checks. We get a big smile just thinking about it and it inspires us to think of what we can do.

Acts of random kindness are extremely important in rebuilding and reconnecting. They form a sense of balance and harmony and provide hope. They remind us to return to our normal, everyday human kindness. In these troubled times when violence is all around us, kindness connects with an immense powerfulness. It empowers everyone cross-culturally, economically and socially.

From the four guardian angels who rescued Reginald Denny, the truck driver beaten so viciously in the L.A. riots, to the neighbors who brought their brooms to help clean up the area, the message says, "Stop in the name of love." It is the action or movement added to the feelings of love that make a difference. Every action has significance, whether heroic or simply thoughtful. Acts of kindness provide the power to turn things around.

Here are some ideas to get you started on a goodness guerrilla campaign:

- Leave coins in someone's garden — this was reported to have been done with gold coins in the south of London.
- Sweep someone's driveway when he's not looking.
- Pay someone else's bill and disappear before she can thank you.
- Buy a doll for a homeless child and attach a nice note.
- Clean up the weeds in a shut-in's yard and water the plants if they need it.
- Join in when your community has a day to clean up gang graffiti.
- Pick up someone's newspaper that was thrown in the street by mistake and deposit it on his doorstep.

- Let someone in on the freeway.
- If you know of a person living on a fixed income, secretly sneak her your discount coupons.
- Return kind words for negative as often as possible.
- Forgive people their imperfections at every opportunity.
- Make yourself and someone else laugh.
- Make at least three positive affirmations of another human being per day. If you are in the habit of appreciating people, it will raise your awareness level of the joyfulness in your own life.
- If you are religious, affirm your faith each day.
- Never miss the chance to say thank you, even for the tiniest of good things.
- Give the world the gift of your quiet competence today. Do your job. Do it well. Do it with joy and all your artistry.
- Forgive! It isn't always possible to forget a transgression but it's always possible to forgive one.
- Donate blood.
- Carry stamps with you. When you hear someone talk appreciatively about someone else, ask them if they'd like to send them a quick note of appreciation. We are often quick to criticize but slow to appreciate.

- Never give up on anybody. Miracles happen every day. Sharpen your visual perception by looking for progress, no matter how small.
- Be respectful to public employees. Thank them for helping your community and tell them you appreciate what they are doing. Brighten their day with a joke or pun and warm them with a smile.

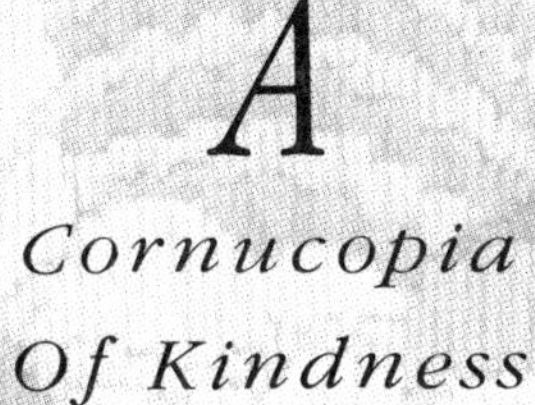

A Cornucopia Of Kindness

Suspecting The Best Of Each Other Until Proven Wrong

Charlie O'Connor is a goodness guerrilla. His official title is school crossing guard, but he is more like a guardian angel.

O'Connor works at the intersection of Grant and Creskill Avenues in Dumont, New Jersey. He protects, loves, cheers and supports everyone who passes him in front of Grant Avenue Elementary School. But you behave yourself in his territory or face his wrath. "Easy! This is a school zone!" he shouts. Everyone feels safe in O'Connor's domain.

O'Connor has been many things including a baseball, football and hockey coach, and a warehouse manager. None of these jobs compare to the act of kindness he's provided on his corner every school day for the last decade. His $8-per-hour wage does not nearly begin to compensate him for cheerfully greeting everyone by name and for including them under his umbrella of love and safety. He gives each passerby a wave and a nod, deemed very good luck for the day. Each child even gets a dollar on their birthday. Children of all ages know him as an institution of love.

Fighting The Dark Side Of The Force With The 8-To-1 Ratio And The 2-For-1 Rule

In the movie *Star Wars,* the Force was the power of the universe. Hero Luke Skywalker used the good side of the Force. Darth Vader used the dark side of the Force to perpetuate evil.

Unfortunately, negativity has a lot of power. Business studies show there's an average of eight negative complaints to every positive comment. That's the the 8-to-1 ratio. How does that statistic compare with your behavior? Many of us have experienced it. For instance, a clerk in a department store is busy talking to her coworker, so she can't help us. When we finally get her attention, she's curt, even rude and not at all helpful. Her rudeness finally crosses the line and we demand to see the manager.

Has this ever happened to you? On the reverse side, let us tell you a happy event which occurred to us in a Home Depot store in Sacramento. We were seeking a certain plumbing fixture for our new house, then under construction. The young man behind the special order desk called the factory and found that he could order it for us but it would take six weeks to get. We needed it that week.

"Not to worry!" he said, calling one of their competitors.

He called many places until he found a supplier who had the exact fixtures we need in stock.

The clerk said, "It's going to cost a bit more, but at least you'll have them in time!"

Now that was five-star service, wasn't it? Of course we thanked him profusely.

We were on our way out to the parking lot when we remembered the 8-to-1 rule. Meladee said to me, "Someone ought to write his boss a letter, huh?"

"I'll do that, but I'll go one better!" I said with a gleam in my eye.

We went back into Home Depot, asked to see the manager, and commended him for having the wisdom to hire Jerry and extolled Jerry's virtues. We followed that with a certificate of appreciation we printed on our computer and sent it to Jerry, complete with blue ribbon and fancy seal. All we spent was a half-hour out of our lives to show Jerry our appreciation for saving us hours of time and aggravation.

Can you look at your 8-to-1 ratio? How are you doing?

Two-For-One Rule

When frustration runs high in business and family relationships, it is easy to dump on someone by exploding with every poor choice the person has made in the last ten years.

If you're hit with this dark force, simply remind the attacker that you are willing to listen to what they have to say, but you expect them to give you two positive attributes for every negative one.

If you find yourself dumping on someone for no good reason, remember the two-for-one rule. Be open to the issues and balance negative powers with the healing powers of positivity.

If we don't like the world we're in
there is always the option to create the world
we desire with our acts of kindness.

A Kind Word

There are a few people on the planet who are always kind. They see the best in people. They empathize, and see options instead of barriers. My mother is one of these people.

Stricken with multiple sclerosis as a young adult she faced indescribable challenges, yet maintained her sense of optimism and kindness. She has been a mother, an elementary school teacher and a music teacher. As her disease limited her flexibility and mobility, she placed more emphasis on her kindness skills.

She has a special knack for reaching out to those who feel discouraged. She is a consummate cheerleader. It's impossible not to feel better after speaking with her, regardless of the circumstances. If I'm investing a lot of time feeling sorry for myself, the last thing I want to do is talk to my mother because my feel-bad bank account will soon be depleted.

Her acts of kindness are simple but powerful and have lasting effects. She makes reassurance phone calls. Picture an 83-year-young lady, with silver hair, sparkling eyes and an infectious and joyous smile, reassuring other folks over the phone.

To be a reassuring phone caller, you need the following qualities:

A warm, nurturing voice
Optimism
Compassion
A sense of humor
Resourcefulness
Patience
An understanding of the human condition
Playfulness
A love of people
The desire to contribute to society.

If you are looking for a kind way to make a contribution to society, lots of communities need volunteers to make encouraging calls to people living alone, or to folks who are isolated because of an injury or illness and need that extra boost. Call your local community service agency and they can put you in touch with the necessary people.

Sticks And Stones May Break My Bones But Words Can Never Hurt Me

I remember hearing this saying from my teachers and my family as I was growing up. I wanted to believe what they said because I respected them, but the fact was that sometimes my perceptions of what the words meant did hurt me. I know that part of what they were trying to convey to me was that words, in and of themselves, can't hurt you until you put meaning to them. This is a very sophisticated concept for a young child to comprehend.

Eleanor Roosevelt once said, "No one can make you feel inferior without your consent." While that's true, many times people we've respected, loved and cherished have hurt us with words. It's not so much what they said, or the venom in their words, it's what we said to ourselves after the verbal assault. Unfortunately, the tongue really can be used as an instrument for destruction.

Negative criticism can be as invasive as any physical assault because the wounds go so deep that they build scar tissue on the spirit.

One day a judge decided to pass a creative sentence on someone convicted of slander and gossip. He brought some goose feathers for the man. Then the two of them climbed to the top of the court building. Once they reached the top, the judge opened the bag of goose feathers. The wind blew them all over the countryside.

"Now," said the judge, "go down and gather all them up."

"I can't possibly do that," said the man.

"I know," replied the judge, "it's just as impossible as taking all those slanderous things back that you have said."

Acting In Kindness

There are many ways to break the cycle of negative criticism that erodes self-esteem. The next time you feel the urge to criticize, take a deep breath, let it out slowly, and visualize a stop sign. Ask yourself, "Will my words help this person? Will it get me what I want? Will it build this relationship or harm it? Am I doing a number on this person to feel powerful or superior? Does he really need to hear this, or should I let it go?"

If the answer to any of these questions is no, then perform an act of kindness to yourself and the other person by refraining from the criticism.

If you need to confront the issue, make a date to do it when you've had a chance to think through your ownership in the problem. Remember to use words that reflect your own feelings about the issue. Refrain from blasting them with the words, "you did," "you are," and "you always."

Look for opportunities to validate others as often as possible. This act has a powerful effect on your outlook.

Explore every chance to show those you care about what you admire, appreciate, respect, love, celebrate and enjoy about them. The creative possibilities are endless as well as the opportunities to build lasting positive relationships.

The Note In The Casket

One of my graduate students, a woman named Marrielle, came to our class one night, eyes filled with tears. The rest of the group showed great concern. "What's the matter? Why are you crying?" they asked.

She told them that her younger brother, Robbie, had been killed. He was an innocent bystander in a gun duel in a bar. We were all shocked and very sympathetic.

Marrielle cried and cried. "He's been a sort of ne'er-do-well and, as his older sister, I felt it was my duty to correct him. He resisted what my folks told him so I added my two cents a lot. All I ever said to him in these last three years has been criticism!" she said.

Her sobbing continued. Members of the group reached out to her. Two of them sat close by her and handed her tissues as she struggled with her story.

"That's all he heard from me: criticism, nagging. I meant it well," she wept. "I meant to save him. Sure it wasn't his fault that he was shot, but he shouldn't have been in such a place! Oh! There I go again, criticizing him, even in death! I never got to tell him how much I loved him."

Her weeping reached a new and higher level. She seemed inconsolable. The group listened to her for quite a while, but all were feeling helpless. What could be done? She was feeling such remorse about not having expressed her loving feelings to her brother, only her criticism.

Suddenly, one of the other students smiled gently. "Marrielle, what did you love most about him?"

Marrielle began to tell us of his great potential and his sense of humor; about his artistic talent and his winning charm; how she had always admired him; and of her faith that he would have been the shining star of her family had he lived. Most of all, she spoke of how she loved him.

Again she cried. But her fellow student interrupted with a suggestion. "The funeral is Wednesday. What do you think about writing a letter to Robbie with all you've just told us and more. Pour out your heart to him and at the funeral, put the letter in the casket!"

There was stunned silence. Marrielle stopped crying. She thought silently for a time. Then she smiled and said, "Yes, yes, that is the way. At least I can let him know what was in my heart!"

And that is just what she did. Years later, Marrielle told me how that one suggestion had brought her solace in the darkest hour of her grief. But she offered the world this advice: "Say it now. Say the loving things now, before the funeral! We're all too quick with the criticism and too slow with the loving remarks."

The Master Nan-In

There was a wise and humble Chinese monk by the name of Nan-In. He left his religious sect because he could no longer follow their teachings, and went to live on his own to contemplate. Although his home was isolated, people came to know him for his wisdom and sought his advice. A group of his followers built a monastery in his honor.

A man came in search of a spiritual leader. He was welcomed into the monastery and joined the customary tea ceremony presented by Nan-In. The man talked of his many accomplishments and wisdom. While he was doing this Nan-In kept pouring tea into his cup even though it was overflowing.

The man protested, "Master, you can give me no more, my cup is full."

"Ah, so," said Nan-In.

Nan-In's lesson tells us that when we are full of ourselves we cannot benefit from what others have to give us. The act of kindness is to empty ourselves occasionally and take the position of humility. Provide opportunities for others to give to you, and be grateful.

For Your Namesake

It's fun to celebrate the uniqueness of a person who really touches your life with a gift. One idea is to do something special with her name, particularly if the person is a gardener or nature lover. A monogram garden, either indoor or outdoor, can be a unique and beautiful reminder that she is someone very important to you.

What you need to get started:

- A container that expresses the person's personality.
- Potting soil and rocks for drainage.
- Seeds. If you are choosing a garden with flowers, staying with one color can be very striking.
- If you are working outside plant blossoming annuals in the shape of the loved one's name or initials. Indoors, any plant in this formation will do.
- A fun idea for children is to sprout seeds on a large, flat sponge floating on a shallow dish of water. They'll love discovering it. Just spell out the child's name in seeds and it will sprout on the sponge.
- Finally, attach a note that reads, "I love and laugh at the way you grow on me."

Making A Kid Feel Special

Our extended family has a wonderful treasure in our Aunt Violet. When I was a small child there were times when my family needed her support to take care of me, and she did so with great love and gusto. She was single and had no children of her own, but she was a kid at heart and had a real fondness for people. I'm positive that Aunt Violet entered my life to teach me how to celebrate the specialness in those I care about.

Aunt Violet kept a stuffed, white, fluffy kitten on her bed. It was special to her yet she let me play with it until I wore the fur off of it. She made sure it was there every time I came to visit. She planned special outings to the zoo and the park. We went to every Disney movie at the drive-in theater in her Oldsmobile and feasted on popcorn and cokes. She kept a blanket and pillow ready just in case I got sleepy. There was a special place in her cupboards for my place setting so that I could get to set the table in her sunny kitchen. She gave it to me when I got married.

Some of the most fabulous recipes I've ever tasted were in her home. I'm sure they tasted better because she made me feel so special and I loved her so much. Every time she came to visit, she brought her famous cookies or her special spice cake, which she knew was my favorite.

There were times when she taught me lessons of safety, or hygiene or politeness. But the lesson that's lasted longest was the importance of specialness. Aunt Violet taught me how to invite people to feel special and worthwhile.

Did you have someone who made you feel that special when you were little? How did they invite you to feel this way? What can you do today to help someone in that way?

Here are some kind ways to make a kid feel special:

- Smile and shake his hand when you greet him. If he is tiny, get down to his eye level to do it.
- Talk directly to him, not through the adult he is with.
- Use your sense of humor and playfulness to connect with your special kid. Throw in a few corny knock-knock jokes, the old disappearing quarter act or a few crazy handshakes.
- Send him a short personal note with a greeting, affirmation or thanks for the chance to get to know him. If he is very young, print clearly and extra large.
- Take pictures of him that he can keep in his own room. Send him one each week. If you order double prints, you'll have enough to use the extras to make a personalized book. Buy colored posterboard and cut it into pieces measuring 5 by 7 inches. Glue a picture on each board and write a caption below it.

An example is to title it with the person's name: "Ethan: My Special Book." This is where you can get really creative. Hole-punch the boards and connect them with a metal ring binder. The kid will feel very special about this act of kindness.

- Plan an outing with him alone. This allows him to have your full attention and not have to compete with a younger sibling or friend.
- Create a special space in your home for the child to go when he comes to visit. Make it a creative place. Collect assorted "junk" — toothpicks, old shaped containers, chunks of wood, etc. Find a surface that can't be harmed. Stock a box with glue, scissors, pens, pencils, tape and rulers. Encourage the child to create something from the odds-and-ends. Include an old apron or shirt to protect their clothing.
- If the child visits periodically, set a cupboard aside just for his things. Kids like boundaries and spaces just for themselves.
- Tell him stories about his passages of time: "I remember when you were five and you learned how to skip, I was so proud of you for working so hard and staying with it."
- Remind him of his uniqueness, special characteristics and the qualities you see in him. Be careful not to

compare him with others. When you make comparisons, someone always comes up short.

- Be sure to remind him of what you get from him, kindness is a two way street if you do it right. For example: "Thank you for the gift of your special hugs, they make me feel great!" Make everyone a winner.
- Keep a gallery dedicated to him: his drawings, awards, poems and any newspaper articles highlighting him. If he's never been in the local paper, send him a message in a classified ad. It's relatively inexpensive and he will feel very important.
- Share yourself with him. Let him know who you are — joys, sorrows, successes and failures. Kids really need to model people who aren't afraid to take risks, make mistakes and celebrate their successes.
- If you can, commit to him that you will be an extra listening ear when he needs to work out a problem. A listening ear is different from an advice giver. Only give advice if he asks for it. It's much more powerful to help kids with the strategies for working out their own safe and positive solutions to challenges. It's better that you are a resource than the solution-finder.
- Kids need to be touched in a nurturing way as often as possible. A playful way to give a kid a hug is the "Oreo Cookie" hug. Get another person and yourself and place the child in the middle, then hug the

daylights out of him. The two people on the outside represent the chocolate cookies and the child is the cream filling. After you hug him give him a little tickle and say, "Now we get to fiddle with the Oreo middle." It's corny but fun!

- Allow yourself to really enjoy your time spent with the child. The ongoing act of kindness will have a rewarding effect on you and lasting influence on the special kid.

Belonging To No One

When you ask the average person to tell you about herself, often the response will include family, hobbies, friends, ethnicity, interests and those groups with which she identifies.

There is a group of immigrants called "Amerasians" who are the children of Vietnamese mothers and American soldiers who fought the war in Southeast Asia. Shunned in their own country, many Amerasians have come to the United States only to be rejected by their biological fathers. Often they have little education and little or no knowledge of English. Fortunately, those over 21 years of age are allowed eight months of public assistance. However, realistically, it is not enough time for some to become accustomed to the American way of life and they often fall through the cracks when the welfare payments stop.

A group of Vietnam veterans felt they could make the difference in helping these Amerasian youngsters to break out of the life on the streets in which many had become enmeshed after their arrival on our shores. The goal of the vets is to have people spend time with the young people, help them learn about America and just generally have fun with them. They want the young people to feel cared about and to know that kindness does exist in America.

What can you do if this is an act of kindness that interests you?

- Talk with schools officials or social service agency representatives who can put you in touch with communities that have a high population of Vietnamese families. Work with your local mayor's office to find a place where you can meet with people in the community. Discuss your concern about the young people who are new to the community and may be at risk. Come up with ways that people can band together to help them.
- Get involved with a community education system that provides classes in English as a second language (ESOL).
- Research ways to connect Amerasians with other youth in their local community who will spend time with them. They need an opportunity to practice their language skills and establish friendships.
- Encourage them to greet and connect with other Amerasians who come to America to help ease the new arrivals' transition.

See the Resources section on who to contact for more information on working with Amerasian youth.

A Journal Of Goals

There are cycles in our lives when we feel less than our usual selves — less energetic, less creative and less enthusiastic.

One delightful way to jump start that naturally curious kid inside is to observe young children. Uncritically watch the magic of their fascination and enthusiasm. Listen to their easy, infectious laughter.

Buy an inexpensive journal or spiral notepad. List a variety of things that bring you pleasure and reduce the stresses of daily living — gardening, exercising, listening to good music, reading a juicy novel, laughing uncontrollably, walking in the forest, meeting a friend, creating a new project or just sitting. Put a circle around five of your favorites.

Next to that list, create another list indicating how many times recently you've done these things that bring you pleasure. Take out your monthly calendar and make a date with yourself to do three out of the five things during the month.

After each activity, indicate in your journal or notebook if there were any of the following changes:

Muscle relaxation.

A sense of release.

Improved mobility.

Reduced psychological tension.

Reduced pain and discomfort.

Increased alertness.

If you do feel there were positive emotional changes, reduced stress or less pain from the activities you engaged in, consider including the activities in your weekly prescription for health. When you're not yourself, use these as tools to help balance and refocus things into their proper perspective.

Self-Talk: Breaking The Cycle Of Negative Criticism

There are times in our lives when we get discouraged with ourselves. It may come after a disappointment, loss of a promotion, a divorce, or the end of a love relationship.

Ironically, sometimes when our list of complaints about ourselves are the longest, we have the tendency to add fuel to the fire by putting ourselves down even more. We wouldn't think of being as hard on a friend or loved one, yet our negative self-talk takes a physiological and emotional toll on us with a downward spiraling effect.

One of the most positive gifts you can shower on yourself is to stop the negative self-talk and cease giving in to the nitpicker mentality. A creative way to accomplish these goals is to reframe the negative language and recycle the negative experience into a positive one.

Don't follow the example of the student who fails one test and says, "I knew I wasn't smart enough, or capable enough to make it into college."

This type of negative self-talk wipes out everything that's going well for this student. It discounts the fact that she is doing well in the other 12 units. By reframing the situation with positive language, the student can gain a whole new perspective.

Instead of focusing on the negative, the student can say, "This is one test on one day out of my entire life which will not alter my capability or my worthiness. I'm making it in three of my classes and I passed four tests."

The next step in the process is to evaluate the situation, analyze what there is to learn or relearn from the experience. The student can say, "I learned that I need more time to prepare and study the material for this class," or, "I learned that I need a tutor or study buddy for this class because the material to be covered is overwhelming me."

The third step is the action plan that we can create to cope with a failure. Here, the student would say, "By Wednesday of this week, I will speak with the professor about possible resources he may suggest to support me in this class. I will ask if there is any extra credit work to balance my grade. I will ask at least two people if they would be willing to join me in a study group."

The final step involves positively affirming and celebrating yourself for turning the negative shortcoming into growth and positive action. This recycles the negative into the positive. The student would say, "I accept this shortcoming and allow myself to work past it in a way that helps me to learn and grow from it."

Whose Problem Is It?

The dark side of life is being put down or criticized when you didn't deserve it.

A tool for kindness to yourself is to ask "Who's problem is this, his or mine?" Such coolheaded objectivity will be a challenge if you're the recipient of an angry outburst. Stay calm and talk carefully to yourself without putting yourself down further. It's also important to share your feelings about what happened and ask for closure of the incident so that it doesn't reoccur.

Some people find it helpful in accepting themselves and their situations to recite the Serenity Prayer:

> God grant me the serenity to accept the things I cannot change, the courage to change the things I can, and the wisdom to know the difference.

Kindness For The Grieving Process

Kind Words Of Condolence

You have a friend whose husband dies tragically in an industrial accident. You know that her grief is great and you want to say the right thing. How do you express yourself in a note? A family member loses a young child to an agonizing disease. What words can you say to express the grief you feel for him?

The answer is simply: just do it! In other words, don't worry about saying the wrong thing. Sometimes people worry so much about the content of their condolence that they say nothing at all. The grieving friend might then come to the conclusion that you don't care.

Here are some suggestions for offerings of condolence:

- Mention special qualities of the deceased, something you learned from her or how you were influenced by her. A friend of ours who died of heart disease really knew how to have fun. He hooked his motorized lawn mower to a red wagon, mounted a sail on it, dressed in pirate garb, and transported all the 2- and 3-year-olds in the neighborhood on a Halloween trick-or-treat adventure. In my note to his wife, I said, "I'll never picture Halloween again as I did watching Gene transport the future generation of play characters around the neighborhood. I will up my playfulness quotient in his honor."

- If you don't know the deceased, say something like, "I didn't know your sister, but knowing you, and what a special person you are, leads me to the conclusion that she was just as wonderful. My life has been enriched by your friendship, as I'm sure your sister's was by having you in her family. Please know that I am here for you."
- Recalling the humorous side of your relationship with the deceased is more than appropriate. Humor heals and brings levity to a grave situation.
- If your note offers physical support to the person, be sure to follow up on your commitment by mentioning specifics at the time you write it. For example: "Would you allow me to take the kids for you so that you could have a couple of days to rest? Dates that are good for me are ________. I'll call you in a couple of weeks to set it up." Real offers usually have dates and times attached.
- Stay in contact. Send notes, even if they are one liners. People need support long after the flowers have died. Make a pact with yourself to send one note or make one call a week for a couple of months. It's the friends who keep visiting, calling and sending notes who bring us back to life.

- If you are a busy person, but you really want to lend a hand, state what you can do. For instance: "I know there are many people helping with the funeral process. Can I help in any way by getting the word out to colleagues and friends? I have a computer and a copier and can notify people by mail. I have a couple of free nights this week from ______ to ______."
- Offer to be a listening ear. Don't offer advice that she already knows, such as: "It's time to get on with your life; you're young and can get married; or, you can have another child." Instead, really listen to her, be patient and sympathetic.
- Be fully present for her. Don't compare a situation to what you have experienced. You can never really know what someone's loss is like because every situation is unique.
- Special circumstances, such as a traumatic death or suicide, still require condolences. Address the situation honestly: "I was shocked and saddened to hear about ______________________. I can't imagine what it must be like for you at this time." Please don't ask her to repeat the whole story to you. She has had to tell the story again and again, and that adds to the sadness and the stress.

Kind Support To Colleagues Who Have Lost A Child

The most terrifying phone call parents can get is from the hospital or police notifying them that their child has been killed or critically injured. Such news is devastating. Many of us have family, friends or colleagues who experienced such a tragedy and we may feel powerless to support them in their time of need.

My good friend and valued colleague, Ron, was on vacation 500 miles from home when a fire killed his oldest son and destroyed his home. It fell to me and one other mutual friend to find Ron and his wife and tell them the sad news.

At the funeral all our colleagues came and said the right things. Flowers and cards were sent with caring thoughts. After the funeral was over, Ron faced the grim task of going on with his life. He came to work and for the first few weeks, people made caring remarks or put their arms around him. However, after a while people began to avoid him. The flood of dinner invitations and offers of help dwindled. People had their own lives to think about and Ron seemed to fade away for them. Seeing his sad face each day in the office hallway left them nonplused, so they began to avoid him. They didn't do this deliberately or with malice, but they still ignored him. When he'd come out into the hallway, people ran back into their offices as though they had just forgotten something. After a while Ron felt like a pariah.

Sometimes the greatest act of kindness is to just be there — to learn to tolerate someone's sadness and tears and without judgment of impatience. Grief is a natural part of the healing process and takes time. The pain of the loss of a child never fully goes away — time just offers a new perspective.

Here are some things you can do to help a grieving coworker:

- Send postcards of encouragement on a regular basis. It reminds the family that you are there for them physically and spiritually.
- Bring in a grief counselor to help colleagues cope with loss.
- Counsel your colleague to work only as possible. There is no proper amount of time to grieve for a loved one. It's an individual process with many triggers — such as a birthday or hearing a special song — that start the process all over again. Give him the flexibility to handle the grief in his own way. He can't possibly be productive if his mind is filled with sadness.
- Connect her with other parents in the company or business who have persevered through grief. Allow

time for them to connect and support each other. It will be an invaluable investment in time and compassion.

- Start a scholarship fund in the deceased child's name for students entering your professional field.
- Pass out flowers to employees in honor of the grief their peer is experiencing.
- Keep the support coming.

Filling In The Missing Piece

> People touch our lives, if only for a moment; And yet we're not the same, from that moment on. The time is not important: the moment is forever.
>
> — *Fern Bork*

People touch our lives — each in their own way. When we grieve, we grieve a piece of our lives lost to death. We grieve for that missing piece until we fill in the void with something or someone else. This is not to say that we can replace that person, no one can exactly fill the shoes of another, nor would we want them to. We do not forget the person, but fill in the void to ease the intensity of the grief.

There are several ways to fill in the void of the lost relationship:

- Support groups can help you to discuss your grief and walk hand-in-hand with others who can understand your loss. By lending support to others who also are grieving, you nourish and rebuild yourself.
- Volunteer work is an act of kindness magnified! Sometimes the person you are grieving for had a special charity or interest. A way to keep her memory alive is to continue her work in some manner. If you lost a friend who was an educator, for example, you might

want to volunteer at your local library or become involved in a youth or adult literacy program.

- Allow yourself as much time as necessary to mourn your loss. Grief is unique to each of us and there is no timetable for healthy grieving. We each travel that journey individually. Allow yourself to act kindly and responsibly by supporting the grief process, not setting unreasonable limits for it.
- A living memorial in the deceased's name. When Hanoch lost his stepfather, he contributed numerous books on parenting for men to his children's school. His stepfather was more of a dad to him than his biological father. He wanted to celebrate that loving memory in an act of kindness that would bring guidance and comfort to other dads who might need the support.

An Act Of Kindness In Passing

As Wilfred Rand lived, a loving, caring man for whom family was everything, so he died, taking care of everyone and expressing his love in no uncertain terms. "Wolfie," my former father-in-law and my children's grandfather, left a marvelous legacy to his family.

When our saddened family gathered upon his passing, we found that Wolfie had, without telling anyone, painstakingly organized his effects for his heirs, wrapping and labeling every item of value or importance. Each label included the history, price and guesstimated value of the item

His loving hand and heart were evident everywhere. "This is for you, Ethan," said one note to his grandson. "I know you'll appreciate it.'" And so it went.

He had even made funeral arrangements, pre-paying for almost everything, and included maps to the appropriate cemetery and family plot. This made a difficult, stressful and depressing task tolerable.

I learned much from Wolfie during his life. And I learned from him at the end, that one can leave this life with style, grace, tenderness and love.

The Holiday Blues — Missing A Loved One

Holidays can be joyless when you're mourning the loss of a loved one. We know a man who became very depressed around Valentine's Day because his sweetheart was no longer with him.

One day as he passed the Hallmark shop, the vivid sight of his sorrowful face reflected in the window made him recognize for the first time the depth of his grief. It was a wake-up call to his soul. He marched in and went through the funniest valentines he could find. Their humor lifted his spirits. He bought a big batch of them and sent them out to all the friends and family he could think of. He was able to help himself out of the holiday blues by giving a little kindness to those he cared about. He felt that his wife would be proud of the way he turned around his grieving energy.

Family rituals and traditions can be very difficult without the loved one. If you have a friend or loved one who is grieving, include them in your holiday celebrations. Being in a different setting can banish their ghosts of the past and relieve the feelings of loneliness, if only for a short period of time.

Memorial Tournament Of Kindness

Unfortunately, sometimes very bad things happen to very good people. Kenny was an outstanding athlete and scholar in a small community. He had an endearing personality and an infectious sense of humor. People liked to be near him. After college, Kenny entered the business world. Despite a successful career, a little voice inside him kept hinting that there was more to life than making money, that doing the work he loved and valued was more important.

After much soul-searching he decided to return to his hometown and pursue a career as a teacher and coach. He recognized his talent for working with kids, which led him to a job as a volunteer coach for the local youth football and baseball league. Our younger son, a recipient of Kenny's talents, was deeply moved by the model that Kenny set of good sportsmanship, motivation and the responsibilities of being part of a team.

Sometimes fate works in mysterious ways. While on a long-overdue visit to close friends in Australia, Kenny was killed in a car accident. An entire community grieved when they heard of his untimely death. The young athletes he coached grieved in disbelief. A moving memorial service honored and celebrated this person whose presence touched so many. People touch our lives, if only for a moment, and yet we're not the same.

Each person grieved for Kenny in his own special way. Some went on to see that his memory continues, not in sadness, but in celebration of his impact on the youth of his community. A memorial golf tournament was held in his honor and raised $3,000 in scholarship money for outstanding youngsters. Kenny would be proud to learn that the first recipient was one of the children he coached. This act of kindness supports a living memory of one young guy who made a difference with so many. Bravo, Kenny!

Kindness For Facing Challenges

Helpless Does Not Mean Hopeless

Feeling helpless can be devastating. I experienced this when a serious injury limited my activity and ability to work. I was forced to make choices based upon my pain threshold. Because of this incident I had new insight into the physical and emotional challenges that my mother faced living with multiple sclerosis. This horrid disease limited her choices, decreased her mobility and threatened her sense of individual freedom.

If there is anything positive that can be said about a challenge, it's that it increases our level of awareness. There isn't anyone who hasn't faced a tragedy or loss in some form. Some individuals respond to feelings of helplessness in positive ways that have enriched their lives.

There is the disabled retiree, for example, who, when faced with time to put his situation in perspective, learned really to listen and appreciate people for who they are, including himself.

Then there's the man who drives for the Cancer Society. Though afflicted with heart disease and respiratory problems, he transports people receiving radiation and chemotherapy. He enjoys giving and getting support.

Last, but far from least, my own mother has a few special qualities that set her apart from the hopeless and the helpless. Despite her debilitating disease, she looks and finds joy in almost anything or any task. She looks for the best in people. She listens, *really* listens, without interrupting, without giving advice or analyzing what the person could have or should have said. She models hopefulness.

An act of kindness to yourself or to inspire in another is to enumerate ten positive things that happened in your day every night before you go to sleep:

1. I saw my child catch a fly ball in today's game.
2. I found three new buds on my plant.
3. I got a call from an old friend.
4. My spouse looked at me with love today.
5. I exercised and chatted with my walking partner.
6. My little girl came home safely from the park. She wasn't lost after all.
7. I heard a good joke today.
8. Someone, somewhere, is getting pleasure from this book.

You fill in the last two items:

9. ______________________________

10. ______________________________

Lifeline

Living from crisis to crisis, surviving on a variety of medications, wavering from hopeful to hopeless, is the existence of many who have a family member with severe medical challenges. Some of those folks stagger under the weight of medical expenses and costly supportive care.

Often these people must find quick transportation to the proper medical facility for the sick family member. To help these families in need, a pilot named Wanda Whitsitt formed an organization in 1980 called Lifeline Pilots. The organization is made up of volunteer pilots who use their own one- and two-engine planes to provide free transportation to patients in need of medical care. As the name of the organization implies, they are literally the lifeline to the critically ill person because of the speed at which they can transport a patient to a care facility.

Whitsitt, a mother of four and a volunteer for the local PTA, Red Cross and Girl Scouts, first became involved flying patients after a call to volunteer her time to local and state social service agents. She discovered then that there was a demand for pilots to transport patients to hospitals in other cities and states.

"When I started Lifeline over 12 years ago, my goal was to find a way for Illinois pilots to use their skills when the state needed disaster relief or support in medical emergencies," said Whitsitt, who has been inducted into the Illinois Aviation Hall of Fame for her leadership in bringing the group together.

Lifeline began with six missions in the state of Illinois. Last year, it flew over 180 missions in 22 states. There are plans for a central dispatch center, aptly dubbed The Air Care Alliance, to coordinate the efforts of all the groups nationwide.

The code of Lifeline's "kindness captains" is one of heartfelt generosity. One pilot informed a family who he was transporting during the holidays that Santa had visited his plane just before they arrived, leaving a Christmas tree and presents for each child. Lifeline pilots also operate with quiet competence. To date, the group has a perfect safety record.

Whitsitt has experienced every task in the Lifeline organization, including helping families and her volunteers deal with the loss of those whose stories didn't have happy endings. Her dream is a toll-free switchboard that will someday coordinate individuals and families with healthcare agencies around the country.

See Resources section for information on Lifeline Pilots.

Maid For A Month

Throughout our lives we have been touched by many wonderful friends who have faced the physical and emotional challenges of cancer. We've observed some unique acts of kindness performed on their behalf and had the life-enriching opportunity to participate in many of them.

If you have ever been stricken with a serious illness, you know that routine chores, such as housekeeping and doing laundry, become impossible. Living in a dirty, messy and unorganized house can be very discouraging.

When our friend Jodi fell ill, a special group of friends got together to see if we could find creative ways to support her. Out of our brainstorming "maid for a month" was born. We all pitched in and contributed money to hire a maid to clean Jodi's house and handle other domestic duties once or twice per week until she got well.

This was a welcome relief to Jodi and her family. Everyone involved felt that they had in some way relieved a very stressful period in the life of our friend.

To get a program like this started, first print out a calendar with the estimated amount of time you'll need the maid. Attach a letter that reads something like this:

Dear ____________________:

As you know, __________________, is quite ill. A special act of kindness that a few of us are supporting is "maid for a month." Even though you have a busy schedule, this kindness is quite easy to participate in. Most importantly, it will remove a great burden from our friend and her family.

We have invited 40 friends to contribute $5.00 or more toward the project. The maid will come once or twice a week as necessary to do what it takes to fill in where ___ needs assistance.

If you'd like to be part of "____________ angels," please send us $5.00 or more in the enclosed self-addressed envelope. We'll let ____________ know that you're one of her guardian angels.

If you can think of any other way to provide support, please let us know. If we all put our heads and hearts together, miracles can happen.

Healing Tapes

Recovering from a prolonged illness or a serious injury can prove to be a lonely, isolated experience. Often the stress of the physical challenge is so encompassing that the person loses hope of ever getting better. The result is a vicious cycle of self-defeat that prevents healing.

As a friend you can help her break the cycle by periodically sending notes or cards with encouraging messages. This act of kindness reminds the person that you haven't forgotten her or her plight and elevates her mood which in turn helps her to heal.

You can go a step further and send the person cassette tapes specially designed to promote healing and recovery. Dr. Emmett E. Miller has a series of reasonably-priced tapes using guided imagery and music to help patients before, during and after surgery. (See Resources section for ordering information.) These tapes teach the patient: pre-surgical techniques; how to minimize complications; ways to enhance the healing response; and how to control post-operative pain.

The gift will increase the person's sense of power and ability to overcome her illness. The tapes cost about the same as a flower arrangement and last longer.

If you act on this kindness, it's fun to send a note with the tapes reminding the person to talk tenderly to her inner child. Remember to be comforting and include the reassurance of humor. Ask her to speak with her inner child in the same safe and caring manner she would to a trusting child. Suggest that she says something like this:

> I know that this medical procedure may be frightening to you. You've taken great care to find a doctor you trust. Don't worry! Everything will turn out for the best. I'll be with you. You'll get a little better every day.

There ain't much fun in medicine,
but there's a heck of a lot of medicine in fun.
— *Josh Billings*

Comfort Quilt

Cancer is a painful, debilitating disease that friends and loved ones agonize, sometimes in vain, over ways to provide a measure of comfort from the suffering.

A beloved substitute teacher, who had worked in the school district where I was employed, was stricken with cancer. Many people loved her and wanted to do something to ease her agony. The teachers and office staff got together and came up with the idea of making a comfort quilt. (See the back of the book for instructions).

After the materials were purchased, we sent out the following letter to people we thought would like to help:

> Dear ______________________:
>
> If you've ever wanted to help in the healing process of a dear friend and co-worker but didn't know what to do or say, here's your chance. Take one of the following quilt squares and decorate, initial and write your name on it and get it back to us by (date). Don't worry about your artistic abilities. Any attempt will be appreciated.
>
> A $2.00 donation will help cover the costs of materials and pay for a local seamstress to stitch the squares into a beautiful quilt.
>
> Once completed, this will be a gift that goes on comforting every day. Here are some things to help you get started:

- Use crayons to trace a picture from a coloring book.
- Write out an inspirational quote.
- Have one of your students draw something for you.
- Write a joke or silly saying that might bring a smile to their lips.

There is great power in numbers and in creative, caring individuals. You're one of them. Please join us in this gift of comfort.

I can't CURE, but I can CARE!

Acts Of Kindness To Community

Troubled Times — Troubled Kids

Troubled kids can be defined as those who are physically or emotionally at risk. It might be the kid who acts out his frustrations violently. Maybe it is the kid with a learning disability who can't keep up with class readings. Or maybe it is the child who has what no one his age should have, a life-threatening illness. Every community has its share of at-risk kids who might be lost if no one takes action.

Carolyn Liebig is the local school district bus driver. A 30-year veteran, she knows nearly every kid in the community and has driven most of their parents. Nothing much gets past her. She believes in the direct approach. Her advice may be blunt, but everyone hears the love and concern in her voice and sees the sparkle in her merry eyes and they listen!

Liebig also cares enough about kids to help with accountability. She will tell a kid to get to school, or tell them to knock-it-off in no uncertain terms if they are acting inappropriately or unsafely. Many times kids have heard the "I care about you, and I'm watching you!" speech.

We need the Liebigs in this world because they make a difference. Although we may not seek the same style or approach, what they do is of vital importance to every community. As much as youth will challenge boundaries, they also seek them. Folks like Liebig see young people on a regular basis, and they can be the link that keeps a kid in the mainstream.

Liebig drove Linda to school for 13 years, kindergarten through high school. When Linda's son Billy turned 5, he also caught a ride on Liebig's big yellow bus.

One day, Billy was diagnosed with leukemia. Again Liebig stepped beyond her role as a civil servant and into the role of kindness distributor by supporting Linda in a variety of ways: touching base with her each morning, even if Billy was too ill to make it to school; writing Billy notes of encouragement; talking with his homeroom teacher about his progress; giving Linda a big Carolyn-hug when she'd spot her in the grocery store. Liebig would slip her the package of Kleenex she kept in her purse, listen, and touch base with Billy's grandparents because they were in need of support too.

The story had a sad ending, Billy died, but Liebig provided comfort and support as the family grieved.

Billy was physically at risk, but for every Billy there are 20 children at emotional risk. People like Carolyn Liebig create genuine community, one that is not just a random collection of houses and people. Caring happens one Carolyn Liebig at a time!

Acts Of Kindness That Can Effect Change In Troubled Kids

Have you ever worked with a troubled child? Sometimes these children are shunted here and there, from school to residential home and back again. Having just established themselves, for better or worse, in your classroom, they are suddenly gone again. This impermanence in their lives may be part of why their behavior is so problematic. Here are some things you can do to keep them from slipping through the cracks:

- If you're the teacher, assign students to write to this child so that wherever he is, there'll be a feeling of connection to the peer group. One teacher we know brought in a tape player and gave students the opportunity for each student to send a verbal message to a classmate who had been placed in a residential treatment center. The kids loved hearing how different their voices sounded on tape and they enjoyed unlimited microphone time. The resulting tape was funny, silly and filled with implied love. The child on the other end felt very good about it, too.
- If the child is in emotional crisis and has the opportunity for counseling support, include in the healing

and reconnecting strategies significant others, such as peers, grandparents, surrogate parents and trusted teachers.

- One school I worked in had the "hands on club." Word would go out to staff members who worked with such students to support them in their school environment as much as possible. Acts of kindness I saw were extra helpings of the school lunch, extra pats on the back, hugs, legitimate ways for them to leave the classroom if they were unable to cope with the stress they were under and allowing them in the classroom before school when they needed someplace warm and safe.
- Meladee usually picks one child each year who needs friendship, love and a safe place to be and makes him or her the honorary "office manager." This child gets to come in, make coffee, refill the copying machine and do myriad little tasks. For this, she pays the child a small "salary." The child derives a great deal of pride and significance from this little job.
- A member of the child's extended family who may have connected with this child in some special way can be invited to be a member of the support team.
- A neighbor who supports the family in some way may be a kindness team member. This person can offer respite care if the child has a single parent, by giving them time to apply for a job, take a walk or just rest. This gives the child the full attention of a caring adult.

Say Goodbye To The "Isms"

We believe that deep in all of us there is an immortal soul. That soul is pure, loving and unconditionally accepting. Assuming this is true, can you imagine what your soul would say if it could meet another soul? Would it ask, "Are you a black soul or a white soul?" or "Are you a Republican soul or a Democrat soul?" or "Are you a young soul or an old one?"

We can't imagine that those would be important issues at the soul level. Therefore we think that if my soul could meet your soul, they'd just love each other. All the rejection, discrimination, sense of otherness and distance we experience results from our being out of touch with our spiritual selves and from the hateful things we've been taught.

With some hard work, it is possible to rid yourself of most of that dross and warped thinking.

Do what is right! Be one person in your group who stops the perpetuation of racism, ageism, sexism, homophobia and criticism.

Ways to stop perpetuating the "isms":

- If someone tells you a racist joke or any other kind of put-down, tell them that you don't put up with put-downs of any group.

- If there is a labeled group that you feel you have some biases about, talk with those folks so that you can clarify your understanding about who they are. One of the great principles of dealing with fear is to go toward the feared object rather than away from it. Make the time and opportunity to be with and learn about this group. It's harder to demonize someone if you get to know them.
- If you find yourself commenting or going along with criticism about any particular group, ask yourself what is behind those negative feelings. Is it anger about a particular event? Is it fear of the unknown or different? Resolve that you will not perpetuate the comments and instead work on resolving the conflict within yourself.
- If you have children who have lifestyles that diverge from your set of norms, love and support them for who they are. Build bridges, don't distance yourself because they have a different lifestyle. Consider the mother who discovered her son was gay and supported his right to be himself by walking down a street in New York City, carrying a hand-printed poster that read "Parents of Gays Unite in Support for Our Children." All parents need be aware that when they mock or curse gay people, they may be mocking or cursing their own child.

- Help make this a world safe for all children and adults, not just the favored ones who fit the popular media images.
- Widen your circle of social contacts to include different genders, races, ages and lifestyles. Break out of your comfort zone to include these folks and to learn about them, then share yourself.
- Refrain from assuming that a single parent of either gender must be doing something wrong. Rather than moralizing, support and help them over the rough spots. Single parents, no matter what the conditions, could always use extra sleep, a day off, extra vitamins and a listening ear.

Always do what's right. It will please some people and astonish the rest.

Kindness To Your Environment

Today, many Americans are developing a strong sense of community. One way to contribute to your community is by protecting and preserving the environment.

Carolyn Chipman-Evans saw great beauty in a piece of land purchased by her home town. It's development would include ballfields, a running track and a swimming pool. Chipman-Evans visited her local land-use planner and pointed out that the thicket of woods and marsh that was ignored could be a nature trail. She said that a nature trail could draw visitors to the town and benefit the economy.

She used her kindness attitude to approach the project,understanding that in most governments, staff are overloaded with criticism and complaints and need a positive vision of their role. The local high school environmental science teacher heard about Chipman-Evans' project and contacted her to volunteer his time and his students to the project. They combined brain and muscle power to clean up the area and plant trees twice a month. The Cibolo Wilderness Trail is a source of pride for the town of Boerne, Texas and attracts thousands of visitors each year.

Create Showcase Communities

Some communities send out a special message to people. They feel safe. You get the feeling that if you left your purse in one of their restaurants, someone would return it to you. They feel warm and inviting. When you walk down the street, folks smile at you and they're happy to assist you with directions.

These towns even look more beautiful than other places. It's not your imagination; they are more beautiful. There is more attention to keeping the streets and public places clean and aesthetically appealing.

Here are some kindness strategies for building an inviting community:

- Contact your local Chamber of Commerce and ask if you could get their support in beginning a community beautification program. Ask if they would provide funds for cleaning supplies to remove graffiti from signs, buildings and mail and utility boxes. Ask if they'll advertise the program and give volunteers T-shirts that say, "I'm Kind to My Community."
- If you're an artist, volunteer your talents to paint over or create something more beautiful from the

graffiti on local business walls. Perhaps you could begin a project to teach art skills to the very kids who painted the graffiti in the first place! If possible, recruit them in the effort to clean up the town. Who knows, you might help make peace between rival gangs.

Businesses can make the following civic beautification efforts:

- Display a spectacular array of flowers at the entrance to your establishment.
- If your business has a window display, feature local artists, including the art of students in your community.
- Provide visual diversity to the sidewalk and be creative and colorful with your sandwich-board advertisements.
- Keep your gutters, sidewalks and store-fronts sparkling clean. Plant flowers and trees if space provides.
- Display colorful banners welcoming customers to a pleasing, caring environment.
- Display an inviting sign on your counter:

  Kindness Spoken Here

  We'll Trade You a Sample For a Humorous Story.

  Share What's Good and New with You for an Extra Helping.

We Take Pride in Our Shop and Our Community. Share Your Good Ideas with Us.

- Provide wheelchair access for people with mobility challenges, including a sign that directs them to access. Do this even if your place is exempt from regulations mandating access. Do it because it is right and kind.
- If you have a restaurant, move the tables an extra 6″ apart so that wheelchairs can pass without hazard. Give your employees sensitivity training for better serving wheelchair-bound patrons.
- Display materials in retail stores at different height levels to provide equal access.
- Keep a notebook with a few basic signs to help your staff communicate with the hearing impaired. It can be a rewarding connection and provide a lasting feeling of esteem.

— Shared by Cecelia DeCuir

Making It Right For Kids

A group of fathers from Holyoke, Massachusetts, gave their children a present for Father's Day: a clean, safe park. They joined with many family members in the third annual spring cleanup of the Kelly A. Constant Playground.

The fathers' act of kindness provides a good model for kids and adults alike for several reasons: it reaffirmed the importance of a safe community for all citizens, it showed that volunteer work is a valuable community resource, it illustrated how pooling of skills and resources makes big projects doable, and it proved that a community is created by each citizen's daily choices.

The happiness of life is made up
of the little charities of a kiss or smile,
a kind look, a heartfelt compliment.
— Samuel Taylor Coleridge

Create A Climate Of Hope

When people run out of hope, their behavior deteriorates: ordinarily generous people can become stingy, the kind can become mean, and calm and gentle people can become violent.

Does the child who earns high grades spray paint graffiti on the school's walls or break windows? It's unlikely. Most antisocial acts are committed by the disenfranchised, disempowered — the hopeless.

A politically and socially sensitive act of kindness is to give hope to the hopeless in every available situation. If you can make restoring hope your mission, not only will you have been kind to individuals, you'll also have made your world a better place.

If you don't know where to begin, just look around. In every situation you're in, see if you can be the one who finds positive solutions. For example, perhaps you can remind the punitive teacher that she is in the business of making heroes, not giving zeroes. When an angry boss wants to fire someone for an infraction or a failing, help her remember how much time and money has been invested in the recruitment and training of each employee. Rather than letting the person go, encourage the boss to consider retraining and counseling on better productivity. It serves well both the business bottom line and the employee's soul.

Provide people with a way out, a way to save face, a method to undo the wrongs they may have committed. Start with this right in your own home when dealing with your children. Provide them with options that are not absolute. If a parent offers only right and wrong, good and bad, acceptable or unacceptable as the choices, kids may choose to leave instead.

As parents, we have always strived to find alternatives to grounding. If our children broke something, we tried to teach them how to fix it. If they forgot to do their chores, they couldn't go out until they did them, but they weren't grounded for two weeks. Planes get grounded, not kids. Kids need guidance to make appropriate choices.

It may be true that the weak will always
be driven to the wall; but it is the task of society
to see that the wall is climbable.

— *Sidney Harris*

Acts Of Kindness In Education

Passing On The Good

We had an opportunity to see a great act of kindness and affirmation by a school district superintendent. In this school district, because of the efforts of its superintendent to recognize his valuable employees, the atmosphere is light, jolly, clean, professional, organized, warm and inviting.

We saw this first hand on staff development day when management affirms and celebrates employees with everyone assembled to hear the accolades.

For years, the superintendent had selected two teachers, and two classified employees — secretaries, bus drivers and maintenance personnel — for Quality Commitment Awards. The criteria for selection are: professionalism, creativity, productivity, uniqueness, accountability, motivation and commitment to students and staff. Each year's recipients become the judges for next year's awards. The school district's monetary commitment is only $200. Each employee received a $50 check and their name on the Quality Commitment trophy.

Last year's award winners come up, one at a time. Each reads a description of the new award winner's wonderful qualities and achievements without mentioning the winner's name until the very end of their comments. The winner comes up front to receive the check, a plaque and everyone's applause.

Recognition can have a very powerful effect on people. It reinforces the idea that they are special individuals. Folks need to feel like they count, make a contribution and are successful. When they do, their productivity increases.

This act of kindness can be performed in business as well as education. It is simple, ongoing recognition of quality in your peers.

A Silent Gift Of Kindness

What would a classroom look like that went from negative and disruptive to caring and supportive? What if the transition occurred without threats, punishment or behavior modification techniques? Can you imagine the focus of a classroom going from punishing for inappropriate behavior to the goal of catching someone doing well? How about extra credit for discovering the good in each other and expressing it?

Such were the goals of The Silent Gift Project at Baylor University. The project was part of the Mental/Emotional Health class and was designed to enhance human and spiritual connection. In her article, "The Silent Gift: A Project for Spiritual Health," Nancy L. Jose said, "The children looked for the good in each other and learned to express the good they found. Soon, the children were happier, more willing to help each other and became more productive in the classroom."

It's a challenge to refocus a classroom from the competition of winner-loser to winner-winner. This model teaches the skill and ability of love and acceptance between students, accepting responsibility for self and others, developing integrity, trust and the capacity for selflessness.

Activities and exercises of The Silent Gift Project are as follows:

- Encourage students to give of themselves to an individual, a group, or another living thing, a minimum of three times per week for a semester. The emphasis is on the act of selfless sharing or giving solely for expressing genuine care without expectation of something in return.
- Encourage students to log their actions and internal responses to selfless giving in a personal journal. Support them with feedback and evaluations from staff.
- Have students submit a personal reaction paper that addresses several points including, personal feelings, reactions to the project, benefits derived from it, impact on their lives, dimensions of health that were most affected and any additional comments they felt they could share.

Students Shared Acts Of Kindness

One student sent anonymous notes of encouragement and spiritual inspiration to a faculty member who was not a favorite on campus. The notes were put on the professor's windshield, slipped under his office door, or into his faculty mailbox. Most importantly, the student recorded experiencing excitement over the threat of being discovered and feelings of tenderness when observing the faculty member smile as he read his almost daily note.

Another student set specific criteria for distribution of her most precious silent acts of kindness: the person had to appear needy; and they had to be someone she was not particularly fond of, or a stretch for her to deal with or love. She selected a variety of recipients and her giving revolved around cleaning their yards, washing their cars, and sending them notes, and baked casseroles.

The entire class initiated a grand finale that coincided with the holiday season. They held a food and clothing drive in which they contributed goods and solicited them from others. Students, faculty and families in the community were the benefactors of the drive. They received highly-decorated, anonymous presents from the kindness team.

After the experience, students commented that they acquired a greater personal awareness of others and a real sense of how healthy a community could be when it encouraged genuine enthusiasm for one another.

Teacher's expectations of the project were that positive strategies of learning to give selflessly would contribute to student's self esteem. Student feedback and enthusiasm for the project appeared to support that expectation.

This idea can be expanded to a variety of classes:

- A Friendship-Building Class: for high risk youth who feel hopeless and helpless. Assignments in giving could be used to help them understand the empowerment of kindness and developing their contribution capabilities.

- A Marriage and Family Life Class: for students to experience positive ways to enhance relationships between significant others.
- A Parenting Class: for students to learn, model and practice encouragement and giving without expecting anything in return.
- A School Site Council or School Board Staff Development Program: for those prospective people who might be interested in working to build a positive school environment or climate. Ideas for the class might involve strategies for encouragement of others and catching students and teachers in the act of giving to one another. Researching as many ways of inviting parents back into our schools is a vital element in school success.

— Contributed by Jack D. Osman, Ph.D.

Learning To Do Acts Of Kindness

If we really want our next generation of adults to be compassionate with one another, to other countries, the environment and all living things, we need to teach and model kindness.

Why not create a kindness curriculum for our schools? While such a curriculum might not officially be adopted by most school districts anytime soon, here are some ways that kids can learn acts of kindness:

- Teach them to be caregivers.
- Practice goal-setting.
- Show them the cause and effect of money management.
- Practice decision-making.
- Study the plight of many plant and animal species in today's environment.
- Teach them that they can make a difference.
- Instill in them the knowledge that doing acts of kindness feels good and gives them a sense of meaningfulness.

- Take on a project of collecting and recycling materials. Use the money collected to support an endangered animal at the local zoo. Use the opportunity to expose children to the effects of saving their environment, computing, estimating and handling money.
- Teach them to become buddies with a disabled student. Train general education students to pair up with students with disabilities. Have them assist with and cooperate in learning and social activities. Buddies learn about differences and likenesses, compassion, patience, tolerance, cooperation and helpfulness. Kids with disabilities learn how to be part of a social community, have a friend and be a friend.
- Hold a "Disability Awareness Fair": Set up stations in the library or cafeteria that allow students, staff and families to experience, through hands-on activities, what it is like to have a disability. The experience will enlighten those who have not had the opportunity to be positively exposed to a wide range of disabilities.

Kids don't care what you know until
they know that you care.
— *Jack Canfield*

Quick Acts Of Kindness You Can Give With All Your Heart

Quick Acts Of Kindness You Can Give With All Your Heart:

1. Smile.
2. Provide a shoulder to lean on.
3. Pat someone on the back.
4. Say, "Thank you."
5. Give an unexpected kiss . . .
6. . . . or a warm hug.
7. Say, "You look wonderful!" and mean it.
8. Rub a tired back and shoulders. Ask, "Is this the way you want it? A little harder? A little softer?" Put the receiver of your back rub in charge.
9. Apply a cold compress to someone's fevered brow on a really hot day.
10. Whistle when you're feeling down, but not loud enough to drive people nuts.
11. Keep the 55 MPH speed limit — in the right lane.
12. Say, "Good morning," even if it isn't. Sometimes your assertion will help everyone find the good parts in the morning.
13. Mail an unexpected and caring letter to an old friend.

14. Place a surprise phone call. Tell the other person the good thoughts about them you've had in your heart.
15. Wash the dishes when it's not your turn.
16. Empty the trash when it's not your turn.
17. Ignore a rude remark.
18. Send a "one-minute love call."
19. Clean the garage when it's your partner's turn.
20. Start off someone's day with a joke or funny story.
21. Make coffee at the office — for your secretary, for example.
22. Save the want ads for a job hunter.
23. Write an encouraging letter to the editor.
24. Take Grandma or Grandpa to lunch.
25. Don't discuss the election with your in-law.
26. Don't discuss the Super Bowl with the member of your family who rooted for the team that lost.
27. Send a "thinking of you" card.
28. Wave and smile at a parking enforcement officer.
29. Use just one parking space.
30. Pay your bills on time.
31. Give your used clothes to a needy person or to an agency that will pass them on to the right people.
32. Pass on some good news. Don't pass on the gossip.
33. Send a complimentary letter about a great product.
34. Buy the wine your partner likes.
35. Buy the cheese your partner likes.
36. Say something nice to someone.

37. Consider a different point of view.
38. Lend a favorite book. Don't nag to get it back.
39. Return a friend's favorite book.
40. Let your partner win at golf.
41. Let your partner win at tennis.
42. Play catch with a little kid.
43. Help someone figure out a solution instead of giving advice.
44. Take a box of homemade cookies to work. Put it near the coffee machine with a sign, "Gift from the Phantom."
45. Visit an elderly shut-in.
46. Forgive an old grudge.
47. Talk with a lonely child.
48. Laugh at an old joke.
49. Laugh at a boring joke.
50. Tell your partner he is wonderful.
51. Tell your partner that she is beautiful.
52. Take the kids to the park . . .
53. . . . or the zoo.
54. . . . or to the snow.
55. Serve breakfast in bed and clean up afterward.
56. Make the music soft and the lights low.
57. Clean the house for Mom and Dad.
58. Share a dream.
59. Walk with your partner on a regular basis.
60. Be the "eyes and ears" for your friends. If you know that a friend is looking for something, or has a

great interest or hobby, cut out every article in the paper about it and send it to them.

61. Adopt a stray cat or a lost dog.
62. Join the Big Brothers/Big Sisters movement. Be there for a kid who needs a caring adult.
63. Keep a confidence.
64. Try to understand a teenager. Try again and again. Succeed.
65. Try to understand an adult. Try again and again. Succeed.
66. Squeeze the toothpaste tube from the bottom.
67. Relay an overheard compliment. Forget an overheard criticism.
68. Let someone ahead of you in line.
69. Catch someone "doing it right" and say, "Great job!"
70. Send a friendly note to a computer. And to the computer's favorite nerd.
71. Tell your optometrist that he has nice eyes.
72. Say you were wrong. Apologize even if you don't think you were wrong.
73. Say someone else was right. Do this with a good heart and a loving tone of voice.
74. Say please.
75. Say yes when you'd rather say no.
76. Help someone change a tire.
77. Be quiet in the library.
78. Type a term paper for a friend.
79. Explain patiently.

80. Tell the truth. But with kindness and tact. Ask, "Does the other person really need to hear this?"
81. Encourage a sad person. But don't insist that their sadness go away immediately.
82. Take a problem upon yourself.
83. Spread a little joy.
84. Remain calm or make it your business to learn how to become calm.
85. Leave your letter-carrier a little gift . . .
86. . . . and your sanitation worker.
87. Change someone's computer printer cartridge or typewriter ribbon.
88. Cut the grass.
89. Tell a bedtime story to a little one or ask the little one to tell you a story.
90. Do a kind deed anonymously.
91. Share your umbrella . . .
92. . . . and your vitamin Cs.
93. Keep a blanket in your car to give to a homeless person and slip them $20.
94. Mail someone a poem. It could be one you wrote or one that is your favorite.
95. Leave a funny card under a windshield wiper.
96. Tape a love note to the refrigerator.
97. Be quiet while he watches his favorite show.
98. Be quiet while she watches hers.
99. Give someone a flower from your garden.
100. Share a beautiful sunset with someone you love.

101. Say, "I love you" first. Say it often.
102. Drop a grudge and replace it with some pleasant memories.
103. Share a funny story with someone whose spirits are dragging.
104. Offer someone a piece of gum or a mint.
105. Give a soft answer.
106. Free yourself of envy and malice.
107. Bring someone freshly squeezed lemonade on a very hot day.
108. Encourage some youth to do her best.
109. Share an experience and offer hopefulness.
110. Resolve to not magnify small problems. Resolve not to minimize someone else's problems, either.
111. Leave some things unsaid; don't shoot from the lip.
112. Find the time. Yes, you can. It involves making new choices.
113. Think things through.
114. Forgive an injustice.
115. Listen.
117. Examine your demands on others. Give some of them up.
118. Lighten up. Find the funny side of a situation.
119. Take a quiet walk when you feel like blowing your top.
120. Laugh the loudest when the joke is on you.
121. Be a friend.
122. Be optimistic.

123. Express your gratitude.
124. Read something uplifting to someone.
125. Do what you value and value what you do.
126. Always bring a camera with you and jump at the chance to catch kindness and beautiful people in action.
127. Send them a copy.
128. If you see litter on the sidewalk, pick it up instead of walking over it.
129. Be genuine.
130. Point out the beauty and wonder of nature to those you love.
131. Walk tall.
132. Look people in the eye — except people who are uncomfortable with that.
133. Talk to children at their eye level.
134. Increase your playfulness quotient. Find a way to get silly regularly.
135. Never miss an opportunity to be affectionate to your loved ones.
136. Invite a loved one to snuggle and lie on the grass on a summer's night while you look at the stars.
137. Take time to talk to the neighborhood children.
138. Look for something beautiful in one person every day.
139. Let go of the urge to be critical of someone. Sometimes prayer can help you do this.
140. Enjoy a grateful heart. Say the sentimental grateful

things that we all feel but some are too scared to speak aloud.

141. Hum the song in your heart.
142. Drop a dollar where someone will find it.
143. Allow someone a mistake.
144. Allow yourself several mistakes.
145. Take someone on a surprise outing.
146. Take someone to the circus.
147. Ask a friend for help, even if you don't need it.

Resources

- *p. 69* • Connoly, Patrick. **Love, Dad.** Kansas City, Kansas: Andrews, McMeel & Parker, 1985.
- *p. 75* • Miles Kimball Co., 41 W. Eighth Ave., Oshkosh, Wisconsin 54906, will produce a personalized photo calendar for only $8.95.
- *p. 105* • Richard Feldman or Pat Berry, Community Worker's Center, 115 Battery Street, Seattle, Washington 98121, (206) 441-7872.
- *p. 119* • For information on the Voluntary Action Center, phone (413) 737-2691.
- *p. 148* • To get more information on working with Amerasian youth, call Robert Duffney at (413) 739-9771, or write to him at 916 Carew Street, Springfield, Massachusetts 01104.
- *p. 174* • Lifeline Pilots, Route 4, Box 150, Olney, Illnois 60450.
- *p. 177* • Healing tapes can be ordered from: Dr. Emmett E. Miller, P.O. Box W, Stanford, California 94309, (415) 328-7172.
- *p. 201* • Nancy L. Jose, "The Silent Gift: A Project for Spiritual Health." *Journal of School Health,* (February 1987), 72-73.

Directions For Making A Comfort Quilt

You'll need the following sewing supplies: Matching cotton thread; scissors; a sewing machine; measuring tape; a yardstick; a pencil; diaper safety pins; 62″ by 78″ bonded, medium-weight batting; 6 yards of flannel backing material; a large-eyed quilting needle, embroidery floss; and 6 yards of muslin.

1. Cut muslin into 30 squares measuring 13″ by 13″. Leave a ½″ seam allowance around the squares. You will need approximately 6 yards of material.

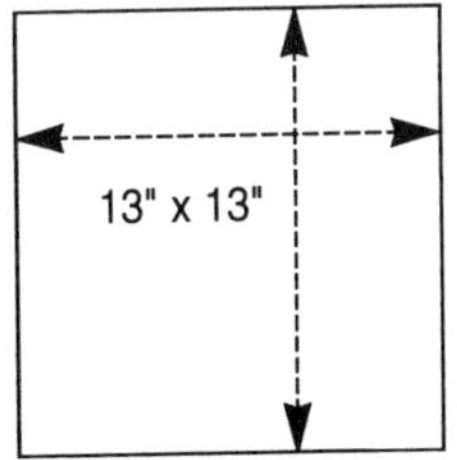

2. Decorate squares using crayons (cover and press crayon drawings to set colors), fabric paint, appliques or embroidery.

3. Arrange squares five rows across and six rows down.

1	2	3	4	5
6	7	8	9	10
11	12	13	14	15
16	17	18	19	20
21	22	23	24	25
26	27	28	29	30

4. Sew blocks together using a ½″ seam allowance for each block. Turn over and press seams flat.

5. Lay out the backing fabric on a large table.

6. Lay the quilt top on the backing fabric with right sides together. Stretch and smooth out the top and pin. Trim away excess fabric.

7. Stitch around all four sides of the quilt leaving a 30″ opening in the middle of one long side. (Don't turn the quilt right side out.)

8. Lay the quilt on top of the batting. Smooth and trim the batting to the same size as the quilt top.

9. Roll the corners and sides tightly to keep the batting in place as you roll toward the opening. Start in the corner opposite the opening.

10. Turn quilt right side out and unroll carefully with layers together.

11. Slipstitch the opening shut.

12. Pin quilt with diaper safety pins at the juncture of each square.

13. Tie the quilt using a large-eyed, curved quilting needle and embroidery floss. With your fingers, poke in the floss with the needle, pull out the other side and tie and double knot.

About The Authors

Meladee McCarty is a great tracker, finder and creator of acts of kindness. A special education program specialist for the Sacramento County Office of Education, she has extensive experience educating children with severe physical, emotional and behavioral challenges. She pioneered the development of effective, full-inclusion special education programs, and has spoken at numerous conventions, meetings, staff development programs and programs for parents.

Meladee speaks about the power of kindness — in the workplace, in the home, in the school — and how systematically planning acts of kindness changes both giver and receiver.

Hanoch McCarty is another great innovative kindness finder and creator. He has been speaking professionally for over 27 years all over the world. He is the president of Hanoch McCarty & Associates, a seminar and training company that helps organizations and individuals reach their goals and achieve their fullest potential congruent with their highest integrity.

Hanoch conducts seminars and on-site training for corporations, government agencies, school districts, parents' groups and professional associations. He has delivered keynote addresses at hundreds of national, regional, statewide and local conventions and meetings. He has received many standing ovations for his exciting, unique style and thought-provoking messages.

Hanoch creates *custom-designed* presentations for his audience to specifically address its concerns, needs and special experiences. He has a wide variety of tape programs, video trainings and books available.

If you would like to receive information about Meladee's programs, or to receive a brochure and a free demo tape describing Hanoch's work, please call 1-800-231-7353 or write P.O. Box 66, Galt, California 95632.

Create A Kindness Revolution!

Mail us a letter or postcard and in it share with us an act of kindness you performed, witnessed, thought of or read about. Describe the act as clearly as you can and, with your permission, we'll use it in our next newsletter or future book on kindness. It will be your contribution to a kinder world.

Send your kind story to us at the following address:

Meladee and Hanoch McCarty
P.O. Box 66
Galt, California 95632

We will make sure to credit you for your contribution so be certain to print your name, address and phone number on your letter so that we may do so correctly. Thank you and together, let's keep the kindness flowing and growing!

Yours in kindness,
Meladee and Hanoch

Books To Set Your Spirit Free

Chicken Soup For The Soul

101 Stories To Open The Heart And Rekindle The Spirit

Jack Canfield and Mark Victor Hansen

Here is a treasury of 101 stories collected by two of America's best-loved inspirational speakers. Metaphors for life's deep and profound truths, these stories provide models for what is possible, give us permission to be more fully human, and illuminate and clarify the path we walk. Just what the doctor ordered to heal your soul and put a smile on your face.

Code 262X **$12.00**

Weekends

Great Ideas For Memorable Adventures

Hanoch McCarty and Sidney B. Simon

No more boring weekends! Here are 52 creative, innovative ideas for making your Saturday nights outstanding. And many of them don't cost a cent. With chapters on Friday nights and Sundays, everyone will find just the right ideas to get renewed, refreshed and recharged for those busy days at work. A gift book sure to delight!

Code 3006 .... **$10.00**